DISRUPTIONS

David L. Williams

MONTAG

First Montag Press E-Book and Paperback Original Edition June 2021

Montag Press ISBN: 978-1-940233-91-8
Design © 2021 Amit Dey

Montag Press Team:
Cover: MaDora Frey
Editor: Charlie Franco
Artwork: MaDora Frey, "Exo In Situ #3250", Commission for the Katonah Museum of Art, 2016

A Montag Press Book
www.montagpress.com
Montag Press
777 Morton Street, Unit B
San Francisco CA 94129 USA

Montag Press, the burning book with the hatchet cover, the skewed word mark and the portrayal of the long-suffering fireman mascot are trademarks of Montag Press.

Printed & Digitally Originated in the United States of America
10 9 8 7 6 5 4 3 2 1

Disruptions:
A collection of fantasy, horror, and
science-fiction plays about the little interruptions
that change everything.

"In these gripping plays time is slippery and settings, even when they appear normal, never really are. Characters must confront and sometimes do battle with ghosts, aliens, AIs and monsters (of every sort), while reconciling themselves with past and present losses. The plots are wonderfully compelling, but the moral dilemmas the characters face are even more so and it's in that space of reckoning that David L. Williams' vast talents are most profoundly felt."

— Teri Youmans,
author of *Becoming Lyla Dore*

"At the center of David L. Williams' *Disruptions* lies a menagerie of surprising characters and conditions: the sky that is actually falling, the watery ghost of a dead mother, the job of a bartender passed on by phantoms, death seeking companionship between her conquests, and more. With each disruption, Williams skillfully crafts moments that grab the heart, and the throat, beckoning readers and audiences into the recesses of our minds, particularly those places we don't want to admit, most especially to ourselves, that we long to embrace."

— Charlene Donaghy,
Playwright, Producer, Educator

"In David L. Williams' new play collection, *Disruptions*, there's a multitude of worlds to explore – each highlighted with Williams' fearless approach and impressive craft towards stories both outrageous and everyday. *And a Glass Full of Milk* displays an impeccable dramatic sense of family, letting go, and Riley's sense of humanity towards his ailing father. It's a situation that, perhaps, many of us have endured to some extent, but the story remains fresh and unpredictable. In contrast, *Business as Usual*, brings Williams' effective absurd-realism to the surface. ... [A] trio of bar dwellers facing a pandemic are handed a twist which brings disaster to an unnerving, but honest climax. Throughout the collection, Williams' shows a dexterity as he navigates through worlds of alien abduction, time travel, and encounters with death – executing them with the precision of a writer who has taken the ten minute play to the next level."

— Michael Weems,
author of *Five Fears of Fatherhood* and *How Shall I Be Loved?*

"These are heady days. And the times call for smart original voices that cannot be easily categorized or contained. Enter David L. Williams. With the ferocity of a flame thrower, his writing has emerged onto the literary landscape just in the nick of time. In *Disruptions*, David L. Williams seamlessly melds the absurd with the profound, using sharp, witty dialog to re-define loss and human longing. Theater is a form that by definition must not remain static, lest it wither away . . . with *Disruptions* we have a refreshing of the root; short powerful stories that speak to the heart of what makes theater great. Williams does not play it safe here; there are chances taken and chasms crossed – But like Daniel from the Bible, Williams takes on these challenges traversing a literary lion's den of topics such as death, mourning and heartbreak – and like Daniel, Williams comes out clean on the other side."

— Michael Oatman,
author of *The King of Cage Street*

ACKNOWLEDGEMENTS

Thank you to Nathan Elias, Leea Glasheen, Soramimi Hanarejima, David Mathew, Matt Mott, and Brandon Nolta for graciously letting me adapt your work for the stage. I hope that I was able to capture the spirit of your writing that drew me to your fantastic stories and that I've done justice to your outstanding work.

Thank you to Charlie Franco and Montag Press for hiring me for my first adaptation and then welcoming my idea of putting together a set of short story adaptations into one volume of plays. Your patience and encouragement were integral to the writing process, and I'm so proud of the book we've put together.

Thank you to Dennis Schaber, Ron Wilson, Charlene Donaghy, Michael Kinghorn, Michael Oatman, and Benjamin Graber for being amazing teachers and mentors throughout my playwriting career. I have learned so much from all of you and am a better writer because of your thoughtful guidance and care.

Love and thanks to Kay and David E. Williams, two math teachers who never questioned (out loud, anyway) why their child would want to write for the stage. Your love and support have made me the person I am today. Love to my sister Jennifer, as well, because I'm sure she's reading this page looking for her name. Now you can put the book down and go back to your Dorcas Circle meeting.

Most of all, my love and thanks and everything good to Kathleen and Sam. Sam, you're the best kid anybody could hope for, and your intelligence, caring nature, and sense of humor delight me every single day. Kathleen, you are an amazing woman, smart, beautiful, loving, and kind, and I count myself incredibly fortunate to be your husband. You are my favorite people on the planet and I'm so very lucky to get to spend my life with you two (and Daisy)!

"Listen to me. It was as if an alien came out of whatever it was, and it ... took me with it, and it was ... an ecstasy and a purity, and a ... love of a ... un-i-mag-in-able kind, and it relates to nothing *whatever*, to nothing that can be related to! Don't you see!? Don't you see the ... don't you see the 'thing' that happened to me? What nobody under-stands? Why I can't feel what I'm supposed to!? Because it relates to nothing? It can't have happened! It did but it *can't* have!"

— *The Goat or, Who is Sylvia?*
by Edward Albee

DISRUPTIONS

Cast parameters: Minimum 3M, 3W. Maximum: 17M, 15W

> An audio play version of *Even* was originally produced as a part of Cone Man Running's Cauldron audio play podcast.

> An audio play version of *This Is Going To Keep Happening, Isn't It?* was originally produced as a part of Cone Man Running's War of the Words audio play podcast.

AND A FULL GLASS
OF MILK

adapted from the short story by
Matt Mott

"And A Full Glass of Milk"
Cast of Characters

Riley

A man in his late teens, early 20s.

Nancy

The watery ghost of his mother.

Leon

Riley's grieving father.

Place & Time

Leon & Nancy's house by the water, morning.

Author's Note

Please take any double ellipses (... ...) to mean a brief pause, not a hesitation in speech.

In dark, the CREAK of an old door. Lights up on an old home by the water, morning. RILEY, dressed in black, wearing a clerical collar, is pouring himself a glass of milk at the kitchen table. There is a shrine, with pictures and candles, in a prominent place. His mother, NANCY, is sitting across from him. Her clothes are damp and SHE has kelp in her hair. SHE smiles.

NANCY

Hey, boyo. How goes the war?

(No answer. HE puts the milk back.)

NANCY (CONT'D)

It must be a tough day. You're hitting the hard stuff.

RILEY

Why don't you just go away? Why do you hang around and bother everyone?

(SHE waves a playful wave, but her smile dims a bit. The CREAK of the door. LEON, his father, enters, holding a pump motor, studying it. RILEY takes the glass of milk and walks towards LEON, blocking NANCY from him. LEON looks up and sees RILEY.)

LEON

You're home.

RILEY

Just now. I's at Aunt Janet's last night.

LEON

How'd you get into town?

RILEY

Rode my thumb most of the way.

LEON

Good that people still give rides. You got your knife, though?
            (Off of RILEY's nod)
Good.

            (LEON drops the motor on the table and goes
            to the shrine. HE kneels, then prays under his
            breath.)
Our Father, who art in heaven ...

RILEY

Yeah, I bet he arts in heaven all the time.

            (NANCY gives RILEY a hug. HE lets her, but
            doesn't return it.)

RILEY (CONT'D)
            (Quietly)
You can't be like this anymore.

NANCY

Don't you love me, boyo?

            (SHE gives him a kiss and exits upstairs.
            LEON keeps praying and RILEY goes to him.)

RILEY

Dad. ... ... Dad, I said-- ... ... Would you just stop for a minute?

            (LEON looks up and smiles. HE stands.)

LEON

When'd you become a priest?

RILEY

No, Dad, it's for--

LEON

Has Nancy seen it? She'll love it. Give her the giggles, but she'll love it.

RILEY

It's a costume, Dad. For the party.

LEON

Party?

RILEY

At Aunt Janet's last night. I thought you'd be there. But she said you told her you had to look after Mom.

LEON

Lots to do. If it's a costume, why you still wearing it?

(RILEY shrugs and takes off his collar.)

LEON (CONT'D)

When do you have to go back to school?

RILEY

I'm not, um ... I dropped out, Dad. It wasn't working out.

LEON

How come? You weren't good at it?

RILEY

I didn't say that.

LEON

That's what you told me when I tried to teach you to fish. "I'm no good at it, Dad." So you went off to school. And now you're back? Are you good at fixing motors? Because that one on the table needs tending to.

RILEY

I'm not back for good. I'm just--

LEON

Your mother will be disappointed.

RILEY

Dad, will you stop it with Mom?

LEON

Maybe put the collar back on when you see her. Tell her you're praying for her too. If she's feeling up to it, she'll laugh.

(LEON goes back to kneeling and praying, in silence now. NANCY enters from upstairs. SHE watches RILEY and LEON. RILEY exhales and decides something. NANCY comes up behind him and hugs him, but it's rough.)

NANCY

No, boyo, don't. Just give him a hug and leave.

RILEY

Dad.

(SHE hugs him harder.)

NANCY

He's been through enough, Riley.

RILEY

Dad, Mom's gone. I'm sorry.

NANCY

Don't, just, don't say something you can't take back.

> (LEON looks up and NANCY loosens her
> grip. SHE is making sure to stay out
> of LEON's line of sight.)

LEON

You're, um ... you shouldn't talk about your mother that way.

RILEY

Dad, I'm serious.

LEON

I hope she's not listening. She don't need to hear you say she's unimportant.

RILEY

I'm never said she wasn't important.

NANCY

See, you're not doing good here, Riley. Leave him be.

RILEY

I'm saying she's dead, Dad. Years ago. She--

> (HE is cut off when NANCY hugs him
> again from behind. It stops him from
> getting out the last word.)

LEON

That's a terrible thing to say! What if she heard you?

RILEY

You're right. It's terrible.

(NANCY eases off at this.)

RILEY (CONT'D)

It's terrible that you feel her here, see her once in a while. Because she's gone. She drowned.

(NANCY, furious, grabs him again and squeezes. HE is having trouble breathing. LEON stands.)

LEON

You look terrible and you're not making sense. Maybe stayed too late at that costume party. Go lie down.

RILEY

She drowned, Dad.

NANCY

Don't put him through this.

(NANCY squeezes harder.)

LEON

Your mother is sick. She is not feeling well, hasn't for a while, and so I pray for her to heal. Priest or no, you should do the same thing.

RILEY

I know you're here, seeing her so often that you get confused and ... ...

(HE's not getting through. A sigh, then)

Fine, Dad, how long has she been sick?

NANCY	LEON
We've got a good balance here. Why upset it?	You want the date? It's a while. Since you--

8

RILEY

Since you two went out and she fell over the side of the boat, yeah? The boat hit a roll, and she was gone.

(NANCY pulls him down to the couch and wraps an arm around his neck.)

LEON

You don't know what you're talking about.

RILEY

That's the story you told us. They're your--

(HE starts coughing at the pressure.)

LEON

You're getting sick just like her.

NANCY

You're not going to blame my husband for this.

RILEY

It was an accident, Dad.
(To NANCY)
Okay?
(To LEON)
When she fell in, it was an accident.

(NANCY lets him go. HE can breathe again.)

LEON

You're acting like she left.

RILEY

No, Dad, that's not it.

LEON

You left. You couldn't stay to fish, so you left, and she got sick worrying about you.

RILEY

Dad, I know that you think you--

LEON

You left and now you're back and you can tell her all her worrying was in vain, or maybe it wasn't, because you quit, and so she was right to worry. You'll figure it out. ... ... Why are you here?

RILEY

Because I feel the same thing as you, Dad. I see her too, and I can't change that. But the way you're going about this, it won't work. I want to help.

LEON

How long have you been out of school?

RILEY

Why does that matter?

LEON

It took a party to bring you back. I'm sorry I can't throw big parties to lure you back. Thought your mom's sickness would be enough.

RILEY

Dad, that's what I mean. What happened to Mom, she's not sick. It was an accident.

LEON

No, it wasn't, Rye. She wasn't supposed to be there in the boat with me in the first place.

RILEY

She wanted to help you, Dad. She worshipped you.

LEON

You could've been there
with me. You wouldn't've
fallen over.

NANCY

I didn't worship him. I was
just a good wife.

LEON

The fall, you leaving, it all went bad, and now I'm here without any help. All alone.

RILEY

Alone?

LEON

I mean, practically.

(RILEY looks at NANCY then back to LEON.)

RILEY

I was wrong. Forgot what it was like here before. She worshipped you and you never paid any attention to her.

(And NANCY comes at him. Squeezing
him harder than SHE ever has before.)

NANCY

It is not his fault!

LEON

You're talking nonsense. I kissed her every day.

RILEY
(Barely getting it out)
You never paid any attention to her, Dad.

NANCY

You've done your damage. Now go.

LEON

She sees me every day.

RILEY

Yeah. But you don't see her.

LEON

That's not true!

RILEY
(To NANCY)

It is, isn't it?

(NANCY lets go of him.)

NANCY

So stubborn. Why can't you leave him be?

LEON

You're not feeling well. Go lie down, get some rest. I'll make you lunch in a few.

(RILEY gets up. HE inhales and exhales,
finally able to breathe.)

RILEY

Mom's not gone, Dad.

(NANCY smiles. SHE waves at LEON.)

LEON

Now you're coming to your senses.

RILEY

She's in the house. She's always in the house.

LEON

I know, Riley. That's what I've been trying to tell you.

RILEY

I wanted to see her so badly.

LEON

I'm sure she'd love to see you. Take her that milk. You two were the only ones who could stand it. Your brother and I, even when he was a baby, couldn't stomach it.

RILEY

Since she fell in the water, I wanted to see her so badly. And then I started to for real. Wherever I was a place that reminded me of her, she'd pop right up.

LEON

It's good for you to visit. Come any time you like.

RILEY

I wanted to see her and so I did. But you don't.

LEON

Don't what?

RILEY

Want to see her.
            (Looking to NANCY)
Right?

            (NANCY curls herself up onto a corner
            of the couch. SHE starts crying.)

LEON

She's in bed, Riley.

RILEY

She's here.

LEON

You're not ...

> (HE dismisses him with a wave of his hand.
> HE goes back to his prayers, but HE is
> not as focussed as HE was.)

RILEY

She's right there on the couch, Dad.

LEON

Our Father, who art in Heaven, hallowed be thy name.

RILEY

If you really wanted to see her, you'd open your eyes and--

LEON

> (Standing up)

Now listen here.

RILEY

She's sitting on the couch. If you can really see her, if you care
like I do, you'll tell me where she is.

LEON

She's in bed.

RILEY

I wish she were.

> (LEON sighs and then)

LEON

She's right there.

> (HE points to nothing on the couch.)

RILEY

Right. Sorry, Mom.

(HE kisses her on the top of the head.)

LEON

Is this why you came back? To lie to me and--

RILEY

I thought it was to free you, make you stop seeing her, but you never did. Even when she was here.

(HE grabs the collar and puts it back
on. HE faces NANCY)

Maybe it was to give last rites. You're free to go.

(HE goes and drinks the glass of
milk. LEON kneels and prays. NANCY
thinks about leaving. When SHE makes
a decision, lights down. End of play.)

BUSINESS AS USUAL

adapted from the short story "Last Call"
by Charlie Franco

"Business As Usual"
Cast of Characters

Bartender

A woman in her 20s.

Doreen

A woman in her 30s.

Marty

A man in his 50s.

Place & Time

A swanky lounge bar, night, during the crisis.

Author's Note

Please take any double ellipses (... ...) to mean a brief pause, not a hesitation in speech.

Lights up on a lounge bar, late evening/early night. A BARTENDER is lifting a glass. SHE looks at it in the light. There's a spot on it. SHE gets a napkin and wipes it off. SHE looks at it in the light again. The spot is still there. SHE tries to clean it again, putting some oomph into it. SHE looks at it in the light yet again. SHE shakes her head. The spot is still there. The door to the bar opens and in peeks DOREEN. SHE is wearing a mask.

BARTENDER

Welcome. What'll it be?

DOREEN

Harhuehopin?

BARTENDER

Come again?

(DOREEN slips the mask down.)

DOREEN

Are you open?

BARTENDER

Of course we are.

DOREEN

Even now?

BARTENDER

I'm here, aren't I?

DOREEN

No, I know, but I mean, with everything that's going on, I was shocked to see your lights on.

BARTENDER
(With a shrug)

Business as usual.

DOREEN

Yeah, but ... I mean, you do know everything is ending, right?

BARTENDER

Then where better to end it?

(DOREEN stands at the open door.
A pause as SHE decides what to do.)

BARTENDER (CONT'D)

In or out. If you're not staying for a drink, I've got side work to do.

DOREEN

It just seems really irresponsible to be out at a time like this.

BARTENDER

Do you live here?
(Off her look)
I'm saying, you left your place to come here.

DOREEN

I was out for a walk. I needed some fresh air.

(BARTENDER breathes in and then out.)

BARTENDER

I've gotten no complaints about the atmosphere in here.

DOREEN

It just seems really irresponsible to--

BARTENDER

Yeah, you said that already. So go and report me, or stay and have a drink.

(DOREEN hesitates, then sits at the bar.)

BARTENDER (CONT'D)

Wonderful. Welcome. What'll it be?

DOREEN

I don't know. White wine, I guess.

BARTENDER

All of my mixology skills at your beck and call and you just want me to pull out a cork and pour?

DOREEN

I don't really want anything. It's all just too upsetting.

BARTENDER

Why don't I make you a bartender's special then? To take the edge off.

DOREEN

What's in it?

BARTENDER

Trust me. I'll make it just right.

(BARTENDER starts making a complicated drink. DOREEN looks around at the bar.)

BARTENDER

Was it a long walk?

DOREEN

Huh?

BARTENDER

That brought you here. I'm guessing you don't live in the
neighborhood or I would've seen you in here before.

DOREEN

Never forget a customer, eh?

BARTENDER

Well, I was a customer before I was the bartender here. Don't
recognize you from then either.

DOREEN

I live just a block or two away from here.

BARTENDER

And you never stopped in?

DOREEN

It always looked too rich for me.

BARTENDER

It's not rich anymore.

DOREEN

Business must have taken quite a dive since--

BARTENDER

A little, but a lot of people ignored the lockdown orders.

DOREEN

I think that's terrible.
                    (Off of BARTENDER's look)
I mean, I was out for a walk. They say that's good for you.

BARTENDER

I hope this'll be good for you too.

> (SHE hands DOREEN her drink. DOREEN
> takes a sip and smiles.)

DOREEN

It's really delicious.

BARTENDER

It must be the secret ingredient: someone else making it for you.

DOREEN

I kinda forgot what that's like.

> (A coughing from offstage. MARTY,
> a bit disheveled, a bit hungover,
> enters from the bathroom coughing.)

MARTY

Can I get a water, hon?

BARTENDER

Sure, Marty.

> (SHE pours him a water and hands it
> to him. HE leans against the bar,
> opposite end of DOREEN. BARTENDER
> notices the shock on DOREEN's face.)

BARTENDER (CONT'D)

Problem with the special?

DOREEN

I ... I didn't know someone else was here.

BARTENDER

Sure. That's Marty. Marty, meet, um ... I didn't catch your name.

DOREEN

Doreen.

BARTENDER

Doreen? For real? I don't think I've ever met a Doreen before. You've ever met a real-life Doreen before, Marty?

MARTY

First time for ...
(Cough)
for everything. Pleased to meet you, Doreen.

DOREEN

You feeling all right?

MARTY

What, the cough? Just a dry throat. Water does the trick.
(HE drinks the water down.)
Now how about some of the good
(A long set of coughs)
the good stuff?

DOREEN

Maybe some more water would be a good idea.

MARTY

I'm plenty hydrated.

DOREEN

Or a, you know, fresh air. I just took a walk and it--

MARTY

What's the pollen count?

DOREEN

I don't ... I don't know.

BARTENDER

Is pollen a problem at night?

MARTY

You think it just goes away when the sun goes down?

BARTENDER

I honestly have never thought about it even once.

MARTY

I think I'll stay here. Just to be
                    (A bit more coughing)
just to be safe. The good stuff, hon, okay?

BARTENDER

What you were having before with all your friends?

MARTY

Double Jack, yeah.

                    (SHE pours his drink.)

DOREEN

You were here with friends? Lots of them?

MARTY

Enough. But they're lightweights. Can't keep up.

                    (BARTENDER hands him a drink. HE
                    downs it and erupts in more coughing.)

DOREEN

Maybe, um ... maybe you should leave?

MARTY

Me? Why?

25

DOREEN

Well, that cough of yours is really--

MARTY

I told you it was just a dry throat.

DOREEN

Maybe you should ask him to leave.

BARTENDER

I should?

MARTY

I'm in here all the time. I've never seen you before.

DOREEN

Well, maybe you're sick because you're here all the time.

BARTENDER

I can't kick out a regular.

DOREEN

Do you wanna get sick? Because some creep like this--

MARTY

"Some creep?" I own this place, lady.

DOREEN

Is he telling the truth?

BARTENDER

I don't know.

DOREEN

Did he hire you or not?

BARTENDER

I mean, there wasn't an official interview or anything. Old bartender couldn't come in, I was here already, so I just sort of pitched in. I was waiting for him to come back and take his job, but he never did.

MARTY

It's my bar. If anybody gets kicked out, it's you. Tell me why I shouldn't.

BARTENDER

Let's all just cool our heels, okay. Marty, why don't I get you another? On the house.

MARTY

It's my bar.

BARTENDER

Well, then it's on you. Okay? Let's all be friends. Double Jack like usual? That's a good drink.

MARTY

Triple.

BARTENDER

Even better.

> (SHE picks up the bottle of Jack and
> pours it in the smudged glass.)

MARTY

Coughing isn't dangerous, it's healthy. Something's in your throat and your brain tells the muscles in your chest and abdomen to push air out of your lungs to get rid of that something. It's the body saving itself.

    (The BARTENDER puts the glass in
    front of MARTY. HE drinks half
    of it, swallows, and holds his
    teeth and mouth closed as his body
    tries to cough. HE turns his back
    to them, staring angrily at the wall.)

BARTENDER
What do you do? ... ... Doreen? What do you--

DOREEN
I shouldn't've come in.

BARTENDER
Why not? We're open. That's what a business is for.

DOREEN
I shouldn't've even left my house. I heard they were going to have a stricter lockdown so I wanted to get in one last walk. I think it'll probably work. We just need to work together and--

    (MARTY goes into another coughing fit.
    DOREEN can't help herself.)

DOREEN
You're really letting him stay?!?

BARTENDER
He said he wasn't sick. I figured he'd know.

MARTY
Just worry about yourself.

DOREEN
I am worried about myself. That's why I--

(HE coughs and then keels over.
Dead? Unconscious? HE's not
coughing, anyway.)

DOREEN

Oh, God. Call an ambulance!

(But the BARTENDER doesn't move.)

DOREEN

Are you gonna--?

BARTENDER

We should carry him outside.

DOREEN

I'm not touching him.

BARTENDER

We're not supposed to be open. I can't let paramedics in
here. They'll report us. Both of us. If we call 911, he has to be
outside. If we call.

DOREEN

You ... you're saying ...

BARTENDER

Or I could put him in the back with his friends.

DOREEN

They're back there? Are they ...

BARTENDER

I didn't ask. None of my business what people do.

DOREEN

For how long?

BARTENDER

No idea. The days sort of blend into each other, don't they? ...
... So what'll it be? Out front or in the back?

DOREEN

I'm not touching him.

BARTENDER

I can probably carry him to the back myself. No stairs, no
doors. But if you really want me to call an ambulance, I'll
need your help. So what'll it be?

DOREEN

Fine, the back is, yes, it's fine.

BARTENDER

Cool.

        (SHE picks up MARTY by the armpits.)

Watch the bar and, hey, make me something while I'm gone?

DOREEN

I don't know how to. Please don't leave me here to--

BARTENDER

Just pour a little from a couple of bottles into a glass. That's
all a special is. You know how to pour, don't you?

        (DOREEN goes behind the bar as the
        BARTENDER takes MARTY out.)

DOREEN

Okay, Doreen. You'll be fine. Just fill in until it's all over. One
bartender's special coming up.

        (DOREEN makes the drink. A cough from
        the back. The BARTENDER doesn't return.

(CONT'D)
DOREEN doesn't know what to do with her
hands. SHE picks up a glass and cleans
it. SHE lifts it up to the light. The
sound of the door opening.)

DOREEN
Welcome. What'll it be?

(Before we can see the customer,
lights down.)

CHICKEN LITTLE

"Chicken Little"
Cast of Characters

Prime Minister

The leader of a small nation.

Violet

His assistant.

Place & Time

The Prime Minister's office, noon.

Author's Note

Please take any double ellipses (... ...) to mean a brief pause, not a hesitation in speech.

The Prime Minister's office. In the middle of the floor, there is a large blue object, jagged edges, almost honeycomb-looking. The PRIME MINISTER stands on one side of it. His assistant, VIOLET, stands on the other.

PRIME MINISTER

You carried it in?

VIOLET

Yes.

PRIME MINISTER

By yourself?

VIOLET

It's lighter than you'd think.

PRIME MINISTER

You have no idea what I think.

(SHE gives him a submissive, "I'm sorry" smile, and when HE turns away to look at the artifact, SHE rolls her eyes.)

PRIME MINISTER

It's very interesting.
(HE goes to touch it, but stops)
You carried it in with your bare hands?

VIOLET

I didn't have gloves nearby when it fell.

PRIME MINISTER

And you're feeling fine?

>(SHE shows him her hands and wiggles
>her fingers. No scars or discoloration.
>HE goes to poke at it, but stops.)

PRIME MINISTER (CONT'D)

You said, "when it fell." You saw it fall?

VIOLET

No. I heard it.

PRIME MINISTER

Then you can't know for sure it--

VIOLET

It made a crater. Pardon me for interrupting, your excellency, but I feel time is of the essence here. It fell, I can assure you, it fell.

PRIME MINISTER

... ... Whom have you told about this?

VIOLET

Just you, sir. I wanted to bring it to you before rumors spread. So that we could con--, so that you could contain the information, give it only to those you trust.

PRIME MINISTER

Good. That's why I hired you as my assistant. You understand discretion.

VIOLET

Thank you, sir.

PRIME MINISTER

I mean, we'll have to tell somebody else about this. One of my science advisers. We'll pick the right man. Er, person. Scientist. ... ... What do you think it is?

VIOLET

I'm not really qualified to say.

PRIME MINISTER

Clearly you thought it was important when you saw it. You have to have hazarded some sort of guess.

VIOLET

I'd rather not say. I don't want you to think of me as Chicken Little, sir.

PRIME MINISTER

I don't know who that is. Is that a singer?

VIOLET

It's a character from a children's story.

PRIME MINISTER

Oh. My wife does most of the reading to our children. ... ... Do you ... Violet, do you have children?

VIOLET

No, sir. It's just a story I remember from when I was a child. An acorn falls on Chicken Little's head and Chicken Little is convinced the sky is falling.

PRIME MINISTER

And you think your estimation of what this, this artifact is will make me think that you're overreacting or ...?
    (Off her head shake)
What then? I need your opinion, Violet.

VIOLET

I heard the crash of it falling, I ran outside, I looked up, and I saw that a small part of the sky was black. A part that was shaped ... just like that.

PRIME MINISTER

You're saying ...

VIOLET

I'm not saying anything, sir.

PRIME MINISTER

You're saying that the sky is actually falling? Do you know how that sounds?

VIOLET

Yes. Which is why I'm not saying it.

PRIME MINISTER

You're mistaken.

VIOLET

Sir, all due respect, I haven't said--

PRIME MINISTER

Your thoughts are incorrect then. This is a ... you'll find out that you saw a, a black cloud on the horizon at the same time you happened to come across this, this piece of ice or something from a plane that was flying overhead. It's all coincidence and you've let your imagination run wild. That is what's happened, Violet.

VIOLET

Yes, sir.

(SHE goes to pick up the piece.)

PRIME MINISTER
What are you doing?

VIOLET
I've wasted your time. This is nothing, so I'm getting rid of it.

PRIME MINISTER
I'm not angry with you, Violet. But I thought you were going to tell me it was something dangerous. Nuclear maybe. A bomb or mine dropped from one of our enemies.

VIOLET
That I carried into your office with my bare hands?

PRIME MINISTER
(Ignoring this)
But your idea, I mean, how could you even really make out a black spot this size in the sky?

VIOLET
Sir, this artifact here, this is the part that broke off. This isn't all that fell.

PRIME MINISTER
Oh?

VIOLET
(Showing on her phone)
I took pictures.

(SHE pulls out her phone and shows him.)

PRIME MINISTER
(Quietly)
Oh my God.

VIOLET
That's the left side of it.

VIOLET (CONT'D)
(Swiping to the next picture)
That's the right side. What I could fit into the picture.

(HE stares and then goes to his desk.
HE picks up the phone and speaks.)

PRIME MINISTER
I need surveillance footage of um ...

VIOLET
Sector 16.

PRIME MINISTER
Sector 16.

VIOLET
The sky, for weather purposes.

PRIME MINISTER
For weather purposes. Sky shots. The most recent ones.
Thank you.
(HE hangs up.)
That thing is sitting on the back lawn of this building?

(HE goes to a window.)

VIOLET
It's embedded in the lawn.

PRIME MINISTER
Why am I not seeing it?

VIOLET
Because I understand discretion. We had a tent we use for
festivals. That's what's covering it right now.

PRIME MINISTER

You didn't think that a giant striped tent might arouse suspicion?
              (Off her breathing and silence)
I'm asking a question, Violet. You don't think that a giant striped tent would arouse--?

VIOLET

Not as much as a piece of the fucking sky falling would.
              (Off his reaction)
Sir.

PRIME MINISTER

I'm still not convinced--
              (His phone rings. HE answers.)
Yes? Thank you.
              (HE clicks on something. Quietly.)
Holy shit.

              (HE picks up her phone and compares. HE
              shakes his head and hands her phone back.)

VIOLET

Whom should I inform?

PRIME MINISTER

That the sky is falling? I don't know. My chief science advisor.
The head of the church. My wife to wake me up from this nightmare.

VIOLET

Whom should I inform, sir?

              (HE walks over and puts his hand on
              the artifact.)

PRIME MINISTER

It feels spongy.

VIOLET

Yes. I didn't enjoy that part of carrying it over. It was like holding onto a giant mop head.

PRIME MINISTER

... ... I welcome your opinion on this.

VIOLET

I'm not a politician. I don't know, sir.

PRIME MINISTER

Well, of course you don't know. Nobody knows. I'm just looking for some kind of advice here.

VIOLET

We can call a number of your advisors. Though we'd have to be careful about which--

PRIME MINISTER

What does the story say?

VIOLET

The children's story?

PRIME MINISTER

Yes. This chicken says the sky is falling and then what?

VIOLET

Well, the chicken's wrong, sir.

PRIME MINISTER

That's not material, that's not germane to your advice. The chicken says the sky is falling ...

VIOLET

Right, and he tells all the birds he knows and they follow him because he's going to tell someone important. A king or a lion. Or maybe that's the same thing in the story. Then a fox meets them and tells them to follow him to the king, and they follow him into the fox's den.

PRIME MINISTER

And then?

VIOLET

Well, he's a fox. And they're birds. So he eats them. And the moral is, don't just take what you hear someone says as truth, because it could lead to your, you know, your downfall.

PRIME MINISTER

That's what it says?

VIOLET

More what I've gleaned from it.

> (HE puts both hands on the artifact,
> closes his eyes, and squeezes. Then,)

PRIME MINISTER

There's something to be learned here.
> (HE opens his eyes.)
If the chicken went wrong by telling everyone when he thought something bad was happening, even though it wasn't, then I go right by telling nobody when I think something bad is happening, and it really is.

VIOLET

Sir?

PRIME MINISTER

That's the moral. It's the contrapositive of the moral, and that's equally as true as the moral.

VIOLET

I don't think it is.

PRIME MINISTER

I tell nobody. And I am safe from the creature that wants to devour me.

(HE goes and sits at his desk and turns off his computer. A beat, then)

VIOLET

Sir?

(No response)

You're not telling anyone that the sky is falling?

PRIME MINISTER

I think it's the best course of action. You may go now. And take that with you.

(SHE goes and picks up the artifact.)

PRIME MINISTER (CONT'D)

And of course, you can't tell anyone either.

(VIOLET nods. SHE goes to the door and stops.)

VIOLET

What do I get?

PRIME MINISTER

What do you get?

VIOLET

For my silence.

PRIME MINISTER

It's part of your job.
>   (Off of her look. SHE's not budging.)
What do you want?

VIOLET

Whatever you think is fair.

PRIME MINISTER

... ... I'll write you a check.

VIOLET

No. The sky is falling. What good are banks?

PRIME MINISTER

Well, what good is cash?

VIOLET

I'm not waiting for a check to clear. I'll get what I need immediately.

PRIME MINISTER

Just because the sky is falling doesn't mean that this is the end of everything. We fixed that hole in the ozone layer, didn't we? Did we?

VIOLET

Then it won't do me any harm to tell people that it's happening.

>   (SHE turns to go. His voice stops her.)

PRIME MINISTER

Hold on. ... ... I don't have the cash here.

VIOLET

Sure you do. Right in that safe. There's at least a hundred
thousand in petty cash.

PRIME MINISTER

I can't just give it to you.

VIOLET

Then I'll tell everybody that—

PRIME MINISTER

That you put a tent over it? There're cameras everywhere
around here. I'm sure we could find footage of you being the
first person to cover this up.
(A standoff.)
I can give you some cash, for essentials, but I can't give you it
all. Once you've left with all that money, what
reason would you have to stay quiet? But rest assured, if you
start talking, you'll be the first person I blame.

VIOLET

I was trying to help.

PRIME MINISTER

And you can do that by keeping quiet. We're not the biggest
country in the world, Violet. This, I'm sure, is not just happening to us. And once it happens elsewhere, someone will
lead, and I'm more than happy to say, "Yes. Us too. It happened to us too. I'll join you in whatever you want to do."
But why go first? I'm sure Chicken Little was the first one
that fox ate.

VIOLET

... ... This is getting heavy.

PRIME MINISTER

I'd imagine.

VIOLET

What do you want me to do with it?

PRIME MINISTER

Put it back where you found it. And then come back. We'll
order in lunch. On me.

> (SHE nods and exits. HE turns his
> chair to look out the window, and
> exhales, satisfied.)

COFFEE AFTER MIDNIGHT

adapted from the short story by
Brandon Nolta

"Coffee After Midnight"
Cast of Characters

Taduscz

A man in his 80s, a soft remnant of an Eastern European accent in his voice.

Wheeler

A diner owner in his 40s.

Familiar Woman

A woman of unplaceable age and origin, but with something very familiar about her.

Place & Time

A small, not-very-flashy diner in a neighborhood, late.

Author's Note

Please take any double ellipses (... ...) to mean a brief pause, not a hesitation in speech.

A coffee shop, late. TADUSCZ, an older man, is sitting at a table, coffee cup in front of him, reading a Hungarian newspaper. WHEELER, the lone employee, is cleaning up. HE grabs a pot of coffee and goes to the table.

WHEELER

Mr. Taduscz?

(TADUSCZ nods and WHEELER fills up his cup. Rain starts outside.)

TADUSCZ

You know, you can kick me out whenever you like, Wheeler.

WHEELER

Why would I do that?

TADUSCZ

It can't be profitable to keep your place open this late just to cater to one old man who keeps strange hours.

WHEELER

I keep it open for my regulars. Regulars are my lifeblood. You're one of them.

(The bell on the door RINGS and in enters a FAMILIAR WOMAN. SHE hangs up her raincoat.)

WHEELER (CONT'D)

So is she. Excuse me.

(SHE smiles at WHEELER who nods and goes to the counter. HE comes up

(CONT'D)

with a large mug and fills it for her.
TADUSCZ watches the woman, unsure. SHE
takes the cup and sips. TADUSCZ looks
at her, trying to place her. SHE looks
at her coffee, then walks to the table.)

FAMILIAR WOMAN

May I sit with you, sir?

(HE nods. SHE sits and sips. WHEELER
continues to clean throughout this.
TADUSCZ tries to go back to reading his
paper but SHE is getting to him.)

TADUSCZ

Do I know you? You seem familiar, but I can't say I've seen you
in here before. The neighborhood perhaps?

FAMILIAR WOMAN

You're Bodas Taduscz. From the old country, as they say.

TADUSCZ

You're a bit too young for me to know you from there.

FAMILIAR WOMAN

I have a proposition for you. Will you hear it?

TADUSCZ

You know my name but I don't know yours. Age has, what's
the phrase, done a number on my mind.

FAMILIAR WOMAN

If you'll look at my face, I think you'll realize we've known
each other for years.

TADUSCZ

... ... Oh. ... ... May I finish my coffee first?

FAMILIAR WOMAN

"First?"

TADUSCZ

Before you take me to ... or have I already gone?

FAMILIAR WOMAN

I've caused you a shock. My apologies. This isn't what you think.

TADUSCZ

What could it be then? Surely you don't have time for a chat. I imagine you're quite busy.

FAMILIAR WOMAN

Time is relative. I'm not taking you, or guiding you, or however your theology has it.

TADUSCZ

Not much for belief these days.

FAMILIAR WOMAN

Amen to that. I would like to speak to you for a while, if I may.

TADUSCZ

I don't suppose I have much choice.

FAMILIAR WOMAN

You suppose wrong. Amidst all this talk, what I have for you is a, uh, a sort of proposal.
          (Off his laugh)
This amuses you?

TADUSCZ

I have read enough to know that deals with you only end one way.

FAMILIAR WOMAN

You're thinking of the Devil. The fictitious construct to get little boys and girls to behave. What I am, well, my word is as true as my ways are inevitable.

> (WHEELER comes over, lifts up Taduscz's
> coffee cup, cleans under it, then puts
> it back, then does the same to the
> Familiar Woman's cup. Then HE exits.)

TADUSCZ

Does Wheeler know who you are?

FAMILIAR WOMAN

He knows I'm a regular. Beyond that though, who can say? Maybe he does. He's a sensitive man. Been so all his life, I imagine.

TADUSCZ

How long does he have?

FAMILIAR WOMAN

What do you think?

TADUSCZ

He looks weaker these days. Nothing I can place my finger on, but ...

FAMILIAR WOMAN

I doubt he will see the summer. The disease within him has spread beyond the reach of everything but miracles.

TADUSCZ

Which is not your stock and trade, eh?

FAMILIAR WOMAN

He does not pray for them, only dignity. That I can grant him.

(A low bitter laugh from TADUSCZ
that turns into coughing and then
back to laughing again. The
FAMILIAR WOMAN looks unsure and
not at all pleased.)

FAMILIAR WOMAN

Are you all right?

TADUSCZ

Death has visited me and I'm asked if I'm all right?

FAMILIAR WOMAN

What I mean is--

TADUSCZ

I laugh at the idea that you can grant anyone dignity. It's
nonsense.

FAMILIAR WOMAN

You misunderstand me.

TADUSCZ

When you came in, I thought you looked familiar. Of course
you did. When I was a young man, I saw you every day. In the
pits and the lines, the boots of the soldiers, the clouds from
the ovens.

FAMILIAR WOMAN

Some might think me a mercy, even in that place. Especially there.

TADUSCZ

You say you can give Wheeler dignity? How noble of you to do
so now. Where was that for my Eleyna when she needed

TADUSCZ (CONT'D)
it? Lying in the mud, being kicked into brokenness, dignity seemed to be nowhere in sight. It was careless of me to forget your face after so long seeing it everywhere I looked. Seeing it and hating it too.

(The FAMILIAR WOMAN looks down at
her coffee, taking this in. SHE
looks up and takes a sip.)

FAMILIAR WOMAN
This is more difficult than I thought.

TADUSCZ
Perhaps you should make your proposal to someone who sees you as nothing but sweet relief. We have a past, you and I.

FAMILIAR WOMAN
Imagine I had not taken Eleyna.

TADUSCZ
I do. Every day.

FAMILIAR WOMAN
And what of her next few weeks? Trying to heal in a place just designed for hurt? And had she survived, what then? To live in constant pain for however many years she had left? She might have come to me willingly then.

TADUSCZ
You didn't give her the choice.

FAMILIAR WOMAN
You assume it's mine to give?

TADUSCZ
Why should I welcome you, when you have taken so much?

FAMILIAR WOMAN

I'm here to talk, not take.

TADUSCZ

But you aren't just here, yes?

FAMILIAR WOMAN

No. I'm all over. Wherever it's all over. It wears on me. I'm not looking for pity, but I'm telling you, it wears on me. You saw me back then, yes, but I wasn't just there. I was on the Rhine, in the sands of North Africa, the skies of London, the streets of Dresden, and Japan ...

(SHE makes a motion with her hand.)

You brought me there.

TADUSCZ

I was not there by choice.

FAMILIAR WOMAN

You humans. I would love for my duties to be visits in hospital rooms, bedside accompaniment for the aged, not a constant tour of horrors you visit on each other in the name of God or country or money. You may hate me, but I do not think much of your race either.

TADUSCZ

So we have made you in our image, then.

FAMILIAR WOMAN

This face, anyway.

(WHEELER enters with his coffee pot.
HE refills without asking and departs.)

TADUSCZ

He is sensitive, isn't he?

FAMILIAR WOMAN

So are you. Which is why I come to you with a proposition.

TADUSCZ

Nothing to lose by listening, then.

FAMILIAR WOMAN

This work wears on me.

TADUSCZ

As you said. A few times.

FAMILIAR WOMAN

I have no one else to tell such things. I'm lonely, Bodas
Taduscz. I have been for ages. I would like a companion.

TADUSCZ

Me? Why me?

FAMILIAR WOMAN

Why not you?

TADUSCZ

What a romantic response.

FAMILIAR WOMAN

Few people are more familiar with Death than you. Those
that are would worship me and the less time spent with them
the better.

TADUSCZ

Well, at least there's that in your favor.

FAMILIAR WOMAN

I wasn't just there with you in the camp. We've been in each
other's orbit many times in your life.

TADUSCZ

Which is a lovely way of saying you've taken everyone important to me.

FAMILIAR WOMAN

And you've never despaired. Frequently miserable and lonely,
yes, but that I relate to.

TADUSCZ

This is your criteria for a long-term companion?

FAMILIAR WOMAN

You'd be surprised what I consider important. ... ... So?

TADUSCZ

Are you sorry? For taking my family and friends away?

FAMILIAR WOMAN

Of course. I mean, it was not my intent to--

TADUSCZ

Are you sorry though?

FAMILIAR WOMAN

I ended their pain and inflicted yours. For that I'm
sorry.

TADUSCZ

How long do I have?

FAMILIAR WOMAN

If you accompany me, then time becomes--

TADUSCZ

If I say no.

FAMILIAR WOMAN

I don't know because it's not for me to know.

TADUSCZ

You know Wheeler is ill. What do you know of me?

FAMILIAR WOMAN

I know I will see you again soon. And I know that I will not be there for you.

TADUSCZ

Who do I have left in my life?

FAMILIAR WOMAN

There's always more.

TADUSCZ

What you're proposing ... I would go with you? I would accompany you in your job?

FAMILIAR WOMAN

I would never ask that of anyone.

TADUSCZ

What then?

FAMILIAR WOMAN

We would spend between times together. Like now. You are lonely too, aren't you?

TADUSCZ

You would know, wouldn't you? You took Maria, after all.

FAMILIAR WOMAN
(A little wince, then)

You've always been a decent person. I could use some decency.

TADUSCZ

How do you expect me to forgive what you've done?

FAMILIAR WOMAN

You're being unreasonable.

TADUSCZ

Tell me how.

FAMILIAR WOMAN

I do not rule the things I do, I just complete the tasks that have been assigned to me.

> (Off his mild snort-laugh)

It's true.

TADUSCZ

Perhaps "I was only following orders" might work for some, but not me. How am I supposed to overlook ... all this?

> (HE looks into his coffee cup, holding
> back tears. SHE takes some money
> (from where? who knows?) and puts it
> on the table. SHE stands up.)

FAMILIAR WOMAN

Perhaps I was wrong in thinking you could. All I ask is that you consider it.

> (SHE gets up, takes her coat, and exits.
> The door's bell RINGS. WHEELER enters
> and begins making a fresh pot of coffee.
> TADUSCZ tries to stand up. When HE is
> up halfway, his hand spasms and HE drops
> his coffee cup on the floor. HE sits
> down and holds that arm with his other
> arm. WHEELER rushes over and picks up
> the cup and sees TADUSCZ in pain.)

WHEELER

Mr. Taduscz? Are you all right?

> (TADUSCZ exhales and starts to let go
> of his arm.)

WHEELER (CONT'D)

I'll call an ambulance.

TADUSCZ

There's no need. Got up a little too fast, I think.

WHEELER

Are you sure? I can have the paramedics here in a few--

TADUSCZ

I'm quite fine now. And how are you, Mr. Wheeler?

> (WHEELER smiles and looks a little
> surprised at the question.)

WHEELER

Well, all things considered, I'm actually doing quite well.

TADUSCZ

Are you certain? Have you seen a doctor, because lately you've
looked a bit--

> (WHEELER waves him off.)

WHEELER

When what's coming for me arrives, it won't be a stranger,
shocking me with an order when I'm trying to close up. It
will be a regular, asking me to serve them their usual one last
time. And I'll be ready for them. I find that to be a comfort,
Mr. Taduscz. Freshen that for you?

TADUSCZ

I think I should be going.

> (HE puts some money on the table
> and stands. HE goes to the door
> and gets his coat.)

WHEELER

She's a good talker. The woman who was in here before? You could do worse for company on a night like this.

> (TADUSCZ nods and exits. Lights down.)

THE COST OF LOVE

adapted from the short story
"The Al Capone Suite"
by Nathan Elias

"The Cost of Love"
Cast of Characters

MacMorton
A scientist/inventor in his fifties.

Darryl
A desk clerk at a hotel in her late thirties.

Young Girl (Image/Voice only)
A girl of seven, MacMorton's daughter, who only appears on a screen.

Clark (Image/Voice only)
A boy of nineteen, Darryl's son, who only appears on a screen.

Place & Time

A not-terribly-fancy suite in a hotel in a medium-sized city.

Author's Notes

Please take any double ellipses (... ...) to mean a brief pause, not a hesitation in speech.

In dark, a YOUNG GIRL's voice.

YOUNG GIRL

Hello? ... ... Hello? Daddy?

> (A pause, then a knock on a door.
> Lights up on a hotel suite. A large
> device sits in the middle of the room. It's
> attached to a few computers,
> scanners, and other peripherals. A
> giant monitor dominates the device.
> Another knock at the door.
> DR. MACMORTON, fifties, glasses, reddish
> hair that's graying, enters from
> another room in the suite. HE turns
> a few knobs on his device, then goes
> to the door and opens it.)

MACMORTON

Is there anything I can help you with?

DARRYL (OFF)

I heard something. I--

MACMORTON

Oh, you're the young lady who helped me bring my equipment up earlier. Please, come in, please.

> (DARRYL enters. SHE's in her late
> thirties, dressed for her job at
> the hotel, wearing a name tag. SHE
> looks tired, and looks like SHE's
> been tired a long time.)

MACMORTON (CONT'D)

And I forgot to tip you, didn't I? I'm ashamed.

DARRYL

I'm not here for money, sir. My boss needs to know how many people are in each room. Fire code and all. It's my responsibility to have a count for him.

MACMORTON

Certainly. And with this convention in the hotel, you've people like me who are all too eager to overload your circuits, right?

DARRYL

How many people are in this room, sir?

MACMORTON

One. Just me.

DARRYL

I heard someone else. A child, I think.

MACMORTON

You're a perceptive woman. You heard what I'm working on for the convention, and unfortunately I'm very far behind.

DARRYL

It was just a recording? It sounded very, it sounded live.

MACMORTON

Artificial intelligence, you've heard of it, yes? But, yes, but this is
(Pointing to her name tag)
This, Darryl, this is different. I didn't invent someone and give her a vaguely female name to make her seem, what? Subservient from some patriarchal point of view? No, this, uh, this is, let me show you.

MACMORTON (CONT'D)
(HE flips a few switches, types a
bit, and the monitor lights up
with the face of a YOUNG GIRL,
smiling with a front tooth missing.)
The voice you heard belonged to my daughter Vanessa. She's
no longer with us. Gone two years now, when she was seven.

(DARRYL looks at the monitor for a few
seconds longer than would be polite.)

DARRYL
It's not easy to bury your child.

MACMORTON
Uh ... no. No, it certainly isn't. Let me, to ease your mind
about how many people are here, let me have her ...

(HE types a few commands on a keyboard
and the YOUNG GIRL's image speaks.)

YOUNG GIRL
Hello? ... ... Hello? Daddy?

MACMORTON
That's what you heard, yes?

DARRYL
Yes. All right. My apologies for bothering you.

MACMORTON
No bother at all. Good to see a friendly face again. And I
really do feel I should reward you for your help bringing this,
this monolith up here.

DARRYL
No tip necessary. Just happy to do my job.

MACMORTON

Virtue. An unlikely quality in such a fragile economy.

DARRYL

Good luck with your, um, your invention.

MACMORTON

It's still in beta testing, but the results have been surprisingly accurate. It's supposed to go live at the convention this week for the first time.

> (DARRYL nods and walks to the door
> but stops herself before SHE goes.)

DARRYL

If you don't mind saying, what, um, what is it? I mean what does it do?

MACMORTON

Well, instead of inventing a new person, you utilize figments of data from people's lives and recreate a digital, interactive persona of an individual.

DARRYL

As a, like a way of remembering them or--

MACMORTON

Because sometimes it's hard to let go. I feel it will be able to help those who've experienced great loss. Imagine being able to talk to a loved one after they are deceased.

DARRYL

That would be ... something.

MACMORTON

Yes. My only issue is that my daughter's life was so short, that her data are not very substantial. The system doesn't have many facts or personality traits to work with.

DARRYL

I'm very sorry for your loss. I don't think I said that before. I'm sorry for that too.

MACMORTON

No, it's-- that's not your responsibility.

DARRYL

My oldest was nineteen when he passed.

MACMORTON

To outlive your child is a ... an unconscionable burden.

DARRYL

Yes. ... ... The cost of love.

MACMORTON

What's that?

DARRYL

The cost of love is the pain of loss. That's what my sister tells me, but what does she know? Her kids're fine.

MACMORTON

Not part of our club, is she?

DARRYL

No, but she sure likes to tell me how I should feel. Talks about Jesus Christ and Sylvia Browne in the same breath.

MACMORTON

Covering all the spiritual bases, I guess.

DARRYL

Just talking to hear herself speak. I've no interest in
what she has to say about my loss, but still she talks. I've taken
up too much of your time. Apologies.

MACMORTON

You don't need to keep-- I think you, of all people, can understand what kind of boon my device might be for those like us
who grieve.

DARRYL

Of course. As I said, good luck with it.

MACMORTON
(Before SHE can go)

This was a recent death?

DARRYL

Excuse me?

MACMORTON

Your son. I see how young you are and I have to assume his
passing wasn't, uh, decades ago, yes?

DARRYL

Within the last year, yeah. Why does that--

MACMORTON

I ask you because I assume he was very much online. Email,
social media, videos, everything, like many of his peers.

DARRYL

I guess. So?

MACMORTON

If you might give me access to your son's digital footprint, whatever you might have that could recreate his persona, that would certainly help me with my presentation.

DARRYL

I'm not sure that would be a good idea.

MACMORTON

It would not be for myself alone. I'd work with you on it to make sure the persona is how you remember him.

DARRYL

I, um ... yeah, I don't know if I'm ready for something like that.

MACMORTON

But to see your son's face again, to--

DARRYL

I see him all the time. I have videos, pictures, so many pictures at all different ages, I ... I don't lack for anything like that.

MACMORTON

You got to see him grow up, didn't you? How lucky.

DARRYL

I think I should go.

MACMORTON

Allow me to ask you one question: Have you ever lain awake at night thinking of questions you wish you could ask but will never have the chance to?

DARRYL

I, uh ... I don't know what to say to that.

MACMORTON

Well, I know I have. It's why I created this machine. I knew I wouldn't be at peace until I could speak to Vanessa again, as if she were really here.

(HE runs his hand over the chin
of the image on the monitor)

DARRYL

I'll think about it. Okay?

MACMORTON

That's all I can ask. My door is always open to you.

DARRYL

Thank you, sir.

MACMORTON

Herbert. Herbert Allen MacMorton. You can Google me, know for certain that I'm on the up-and-up, all right?

(SHE nods and goes. HE goes and
types a few lines of code and
starts whistling a song. HE
exits to the bathroom. Then
a knock on the door. The whistling
stops. A knock again. HE enters
and goes to the door. HE looks
through the peephole and opens it.)

MACMORTON (CONT'D)

I upset you, didn't I? All I can do is apologize.

(DARRYL enters and goes to the machine.)

DARRYL

It's not a trick?

MACMORTON

My work? No, hardly.

DARRYL

I can ask it anything I want?

MACMORTON

She, and *yes*, you can. But you'll only get the answer a child of seven could give.

DARRYL

Vanessa, what's, um, what's your favorite food?

YOUNG GIRL

I like spaghetti and, and, and grilled cheese, and my aunt let me try her sushi the last time she came over to watch me. I didn't like it, but I bet I will when I get older.

MACMORTON

I'm not trying to trick people. I'm just hoping to help them grieve.

DARRYL

Aren't you supposed to just accept the loss? That's what the support group told me.

MACMORTON

Jesus, psychics, acceptance, so many choices out there. Why aren't you allowed this option too?

(DARRYL considers this and then takes
a phone from her belongings.)

MACMORTON (CONT'D)

Oh, well, you'll need to separate out what was your son from everything else, or I'll be--

DARRYL

This is Clark's phone.

MACMORTON

You just have it here? Did one of the men on the 8th floor put you up to this? They like to embarrass their rivals--

DARRYL

I carry his phone, keep it charged, in case one of his friends calls. Someone who doesn't know he's gone. Someone who can explain to me why ... Look.
> (SHE takes out her phone and shows
> the matching lock screens.)

This is us together. The last time together, on his birth-day. When I didn't know it would be the last time we'd be together.

MACMORTON

Oh. I didn't mean to ... people here can be so cruel and--

DARRYL

I don't care. But if you can do something, I want you to do it. Can you really?

MACMORTON

I think so, yes.

DARRYL

Then here.

> (HE nods and takes her son's phone.
> HE types with one hand and connects
> the phone to a cord with another.
> The YOUNG GIRL disappears from the
> screen, replaced with coding text.)

MACMORTON

If you could bring up any voicemails he might have left on your phone as well, that would be helpful.

(SHE finds them and hands her phone to him. HE connects it to a cord.)

DARRYL (CONT'D)

What now?

MACMORTON

You just wait. Go back to work if you want.

(SHE nods but doesn't move. After, a bit of analysis, CLARK's voice is heard.)

CLARK (VOICE)

Hey, Mom, it's me. Wanted to wish you a happy birthday.

MACMORTON

Seems like a nice boy.

DARRYL

I should've picked up.

MACMORTON

I'm sure you had your reasons.

DARRYL

I was here, working. I don't know if that's a good reason.

CLARK (VOICE)

Hey, Mom. ... ... I said, hey, Mom.

MACMORTON

You can respond if you like. It speeds up the process to--

CLARK (VOICE)

How's your birthday going?

(DARRYL is frozen. MACMORTON notices.)

MACMORTON

Maybe you should go back to work. This'll take a while.

CLARK (VOICE)

I just wanted to love her, Mom. She didn't love me back.

(This stirs DARRYL. SHE goes to the machine.)

DARRYL

This was a mistake.

(SHE tries to push some buttons.)

MACMORTON

Stop! You could damage my work, ruin everything.

CLARK (VOICE)

Mom, I had to do it. Please forgive me.

DARRYL

You need to stop this right now. Give me back the phone or I'll call the police.

MACMORTON

Fine. I just need to--

(CLARK's face appears on the screen.
DARRYL stops in her tracks.)

DARRYL

... ... Sweetie.

CLARK

Hey, Mom, it's me. Wanted to wish you a happy birthday.

DARRYL

Thank you.

CLARK

I just couldn't see another way to not feel like this.

DARRYL

I know, sweetie. I know.

CLARK

I'm so sorry, Mom. I had to do it. Please forgive me.

(DARRYL stares at the screen, then puts her arms around it.)

DARRYL

It's okay. Mom's here.

(Lights down. End of play.)

DISRUPTION

adapted from the short story
"Who You Will Be Meets Who I Am"
by Soramimi Hanarejima

"Disruption"
Cast of Characters

Megan

A scientist in her 30s.

Johanna

A saleswoman in her 30s.

Place & Time

Midtown east, New York City, a winter afternoon.

Author's Notes

Please take any double ellipses (... ...) to mean a brief pause, not a hesitation in speech.

Overlaps are marked in Caryl Churchill's style of a slash (/) meaning the beginning of an overlap.

Lights up on MEGAN and JOHANNA on a street corner in midtown New York City.

JOHANNA

I can't believe you bring this up when you're paying the check.

MEGAN

It's just a little move forward, not/ a whole ...

JOHANNA

I'm sitting there babbling about making my dumb sales quota and you've invented a way to travel through--

MEGAN

It's, you know, it just works for fruit flies. It's not people.

JOHANNA

Not yet. But who knows where this'll lead.

MEGAN

Maybe nowhere.

JOHANNA

Don't sell yourself short. This is ... I'll be able to say I knew you when.

MEGAN

Well, it's just one little discovery. It's not like I can take you time traveling tomorrow.

JOHANNA

Or maybe you did and we're back at today.

MEGAN

I couldn't do that without your knowing. It'd be unethical and you might run into your past self and it would cause a, a temporal branching that ...

MEGAN (CONT'D)
(SHE trails off when SHE sees
JOANNA's look.)
You were just joking.

JOHANNA
Sometimes you're too smart for your own good, my friend.

MEGAN
(A little laugh)
I guess so. Anyway nothing's for sure yet. We have to test it
and make sure it wasn't a fluke or a mistake or--

JOHANNA
Megan. This is a big deal. I'm so proud of you.

(SHE hugs MEGAN, an embrace that
means more to MEGAN than JOHANNA.
When THEY break,)

JOHANNA   MEGAN
I should get going.   You wanna go ice skating?

JOHANNA
What?

MEGAN
To celebrate. I can't go back to my lab right now, there's
analysis that has to be done and, and I figure with Rockefeller
Center right there ... I've never gone, have you?

JOHANNA
I would love to, but I have to get back to work. Rain check,
okay?

MEGAN
Okay. Have a good um, a good one.

JOHANNA

You too. Thanks for lunch. And congrats. It's amazing. You're amazing.

(JOHANNA exits SR. MEGAN watches
her go, disappointed. SHE gets
out her phone and makes a call.)

MEGAN

Hey, how's it going there? ... ... Good. That's a good sign. I was thinking of coming in and writing the protocol now since there's nothing else to ... ... I know, we can't use it ourselves, but I've gotta do something with my time. I'll come back in and put it together. See you in a few.

(SHE hangs up her phone and goes to cross the
stage and exit SL. JOHANNA, in a completely different coat, enters SL. MEGAN stops when SHE sees
JOHANNA who is looking around, observing.)

MEGAN

Johanna?

JOHANNA
(Noticing her)

Oh hey. How are you?

MEGAN

How did you get here?

JOHANNA

Same way you did, I'd guess. Didn't know you'd be here.

MEGAN

No, I mean you left that way, I ... did you double back behind me or ... were you/ wearing that coat before?

JOHANNA

It's really good to see you. It's been ages, hasn't it?

MEGAN

No, it's only been ...

JOHANNA

Wow, isn't it great how this place used to be?

MEGAN

Are you feeling all right?

JOHANNA
(Finally realizing)

Ohhhh, you're from then.

MEGAN

I'm from--?

JOHANNA

It works now, Megan. Not just on fruit flies. I mean not your now, but mine.

MEGAN

So you traveled from ... ?
(Off of JOHANNA's nod)

That's ... that's incredible. I was just about to write up the protocol for the possibility of ...
(SHE looks around, then whispers)

But you're not supposed to be here now. Unless it's an emergency. Is it an emergency?

JOHANNA

Relax. I was just feeling nostalgic.

MEGAN
(Too loud)
You're here because of nostalgia?

JOHANNA
You never visited your old hometown?

MEGAN
(With some urgency)
But you should be in disguise, if you even should be doing it at all. That's what the protocol is going to say. You have to do that to prevent meetings like this, so you don't create a temporal branching and never be able to get back to where you came from. You wouldn't understand, it's not--

JOHANNA
That's not an issue.

MEGAN
Yes it is. Jesus, process isn't even around for a day and people are already ripping at the fabric of--

JOHANNA
They solved that problem. I know what temporal branching is. I work for the company that ... actually, that's not something I can reveal. And I'll have to disrupt your memory after this to minimize the effects of this visit.

MEGAN
You can do that?

JOHANNA
It's used for any incidental contact with someone who can recognize you. It's the only reason I'm allowed to be back here.

MEGAN

How did they solve the problem of--?
(Off of JOHANNA's head shake)
If you're going to prevent me from remembering this, why
can't you just explain it to me?

JOHANNA

Because telling you too much could still have some ...
undesirable effects.

MEGAN

Because the memory disruption isn't totally perfect?

JOHANNA

I can't really talk about that. You see, I do follow the protocol.
For the most part. Was I really just here?

MEGAN

What? Oh, yeah. I mean, the now, my now you was. We had
lunch. If you want to see her, she went back to--

JOHANNA

No, I saw her this morning. Followed her for a little while, like
I was a spy.

MEGAN

Was it weird seeing yourself?

JOHANNA

A little. It was nice too. I like that former self of mine.

MEGAN

Me too.

JOHANNA

I'd forgotten that this was a day we had lunch. I shouldn't
have involved you in this, my apologies.

MEGAN

It's, it's fine.

JOHANNA

To make it up to you, you can ask me about anything, as long as it's not directly related to the future.
(Off of MEGAN's small laugh)
What?

MEGAN

What do you want me to ask? "How are you doing?"

JOHANNA

Pretty good, thanks. It's a beautiful winter day.

MEGAN

What are you really doing here, Johanna?

JOHANNA

Nothing sinister. Just enjoying things as they used to be.

MEGAN

So it won't be like this in the future?

JOHANNA

No.

MEGAN

How come you could answer that question?

JOHANNA

Because that answer isn't so revealing. I mean, you really don't think it's going to be like this forever, do you?

MEGAN

Well, no. But I thought some things would endure.

JOHANNA

Oh, sure, definitely. Some things will. I just can't tell you which ones.

MEGAN

Where else have you been today? Can you tell me that or--?

JOHANNA

Bookstores mostly. The ones I liked.

MEGAN

There aren't bookstores in the future?

JOHANNA

Not like the ones in your now.

MEGAN

How come you could--?

JOHANNA

Quit trying to trap me in some lie, Megan. Are there as many bookstores in your now as there were twenty years ago? You invented time travel. I think you can extrapolate out.

MEGAN

I'm sorry.

JOHANNA

It's fine. It's ... if it were anybody else seeing me that I knew before I would've disrupted them right away. I figured you of all people could handle it.

MEGAN

I guess I didn't realize it would all happen so quickly.

JOHANNA

It doesn't though. Not really. I should let you enjoy all that.
I'll fix your memory and I'll let you go back and write that
protocol that I promise to scrupulously follow from now on.

MEGAN

And I'll get to learn for myself what endures and what
doesn't.

JOHANNA

That's the idea.

(JOHANNA reaches in her coat for
a device. MEGAN realizes something.)

MEGAN

You said ...

JOHANNA

Hmm?

MEGAN

You said it's been ages since we've seen each other.

JOHANNA

I thought you were from my now.

MEGAN

No, I know, but ... does that mean we don't endure?

JOHANNA

Of course we do. I'm around. I know you're still around.

MEGAN

I meant us.

JOHANNA

As friends?

MEGAN

As anything.

JOHANNA

Were we an us?

MEGAN

I was hoping we would be. I guess I don't do anything. Shit.

JOHANNA

Wow. I had no idea you felt that way.

MEGAN

What would you have done had you known?

JOHANNA

Who can say? It's the past.

MEGAN

Are you with someone now? Am I?

JOHANNA

I can't/ tell you.

MEGAN

You can't tell me. Of course.

JOHANNA

No. ... ... Are you ready?

MEGAN

How does the disruption work?

JOHANNA

It's just a sound that I play in your ear that--

MEGAN

No, I mean. Will it all be a blank? Will it be vague
recollections or--

JOHANNA

Megan, I--

MEGAN

Look, you can tell me if I, if I think to myself, be brave, Megan, just, just say the thing you want to say, tell her that you're in love with her and ... If I think those things before you do it, will it all be washed away, or will something remain, an itch that will push me to, to at least try now that I know that I didn't, or won't, I ... Even if it fails I want to have at least tried. Can you tell me that?

JOHANNA

No.

MEGAN

Why not?

JOHANNA

Because of the protocol you wrote. Will write. This can't have happened.

MEGAN

I can't overrule myself?

JOHANNA

That's in there too.

MEGAN

Too smart for my own good.

JOHANNA

I guess so.

MEGAN

Okay. Fuck it. Go ahead and zap me or whatever.
          (SHE closes her eyes and waits. JOHANNA con-
          siders it, but can't bring herself to do it.)

MEGAN (CONT'D)

Is it like super-high pitched and I can't--

JOHANNA

Let's go do something first.

MEGAN
(Opening her eyes)

Do something?

JOHANNA

Go have fun. Something together.

MEGAN

Like a date?

JOHANNA

Yeah. That we never had. Do you wanna go ice skating?
(Mistaking MEGAN's surprise for anxiety)
We're right near Rockefeller Center, right? Let's do it. It'll be
fun. Kitschy. Ice is so last decade where I am now.

MEGAN

I'd love to.

JOHANNA

I'll still have to disrupt you when it's over, but--

(Impulsively MEGAN kisses JOHANNA.)

MEGAN

Let's just enjoy this until it never happened.

(MEGAN takes JOHANNA's hand and
THEY go. Lights down. End of play.)

EVEN

<u>**Even**</u>
Cast of Characters

Amber
Twentysomething, cute and bookish.

Brian
Twentysomething, handsome and athletic.

Zach
Twentysomething, kind of a rich prick (but attractive too).

Place & Time

The drawing room of a baroque old house, night.

Author's Note

Please take any double ellipses (... ...) to mean a brief pause, not a hesitation in speech.

> A drawing room of a baroque house.
> ZACH pushes a large table towards
> the door. AMBER comes in breath-
> less, slamming the door behind her.

AMBER

Zach, thank God it's you. I didn't know you made it out.

ZACH

I didn't make it out. I made it here. Where's your boyfriend?
Did he get, uh ...?

AMBER

I don't know. We were running, we got split up. For all I know
he made it out for real, got away from ... Jesus, what was that
thing? It was all muscles and teeth.

ZACH

Yeah, and I don't want in it here. Help me with this table. We
need to block the door.

AMBER

It looks so heavy, I don't know if I can--

ZACH

I can't do it myself. Just help me, Amber.

> (THEY push the table and block the door.
> Then a loud banging on the door.)

ZACH

Hurry, keep pushing!

BRIAN
> (From behind the door)

Let me in! Please!

ZACH
(Whispering)
We can't just trust that--

AMBER
(Matching him)
Are you insane? Let him in.

(THEY quickly move the table a bit.
BRIAN squeezes through the door
and slams it behind him.)

BRIAN
Amber! You're all right!!

AMBER
I was so scared when we got separated. I thought--

ZACH
Talk later. Brian, push.

BRIAN
Okay.

(THEY slam the table into the door.)

AMBER
All right, that door's taken care of. Let's wait for him to try to get in this way and while he's occupied with that, we'll keep moving.

ZACH
Keep moving where?

BRIAN
What's the problem? Is the other door locked?

ZACH

What other door?

AMBER

You can't be ... shit. Shit, shit shit.

BRIAN

It's not the worst news. I'm serious. One way out means only
one way in. If he can't get in here, we're safe.

AMBER

Safe to be trapped in here while he sets fire to the house, or
leaves us to starve, or--

BRIAN

If it's so terrible, why'd you set up camp here?

AMBER

I didn't. I was trying to find a place to hide and I found Zach
in this room.

BRIAN

Why were you here?

ZACH

Any port in a storm. Plus, old spooky house like this, I was
hoping for a secret passage or something.

AMBER

We shouldn't have come here.

BRIAN

No shit. I told you that.

AMBER

Brian, you said that when that thing came in the room. When
we got the invitation for dinner from "The Secret Society of
East Grimstad," you said it sounded badass.

BRIAN

Well ... well you didn't try to talk me out of it either. You said it sounded "intriguing."

AMBER

I don't remember it that way, but ... Zach, any luck with that secret passage?

ZACH

Totally. Didn't you hear the whole wall move when I pulled out this book?

AMBER

We have to make a plan. Figure out how to stop that thing.

BRIAN

Stop him? It tore Casey in half.

AMBER

I don't wanna think about that right now.

BRIAN

That's all I can think about.

AMBER

Well, get past it quick, because we've gotta figure out what to do.

ZACH

What if we give him what he wants?

BRIAN

What are you talking about?

AMBER

How do you know it's a him?

ZACH

It. Them. Whatever.

BRIAN

I don't care about ... Give him what he wants? He wants us all dead.

ZACH

Yeah but why? If we figure that out, that could help.

BRIAN

We don't even know what he is, and now you want to go deep into his psychology? Good luck.

AMBER

Revenge. That's what it wants. What else could it be?

BRIAN

Anything. He's nuts.

ZACH

Whatever he is, he's not that.

BRIAN

Are you kidding me? He's killed half of us.

AMBER

And he planned it. We didn't wander into his cave by mistake. He fooled us, invited us here. He's focused.

BRIAN

He slaughtered three of our friends.

ZACH

She said he was focused, not level-headed.

AMBER

He thinks we did something to him and now he wants to pay us back. Maybe it's--

> (A slam against the door. Not a knock,
> but someone crashing into it.)

BRIAN

Hey, asshole, if you try to come in here, we'll--

(Another bang agains the door, harder.)

ZACH

We'll what? What can we threaten him with?

(A low snarling.)

ZACH

Listen, man, we think you wanna get even with us. Is that right? ... ... One for yes, two for no?

(One pound on the door.)

ZACH

Well, there's one of you and you've taken three of us. I feel like you're more than even. You're ahead. So how about you let us go?

(Two pounds on the door.)

BRIAN

Wow, reasoning with him didn't work. I'm shocked.

AMBER

That's not helping, sweetheart.

BRIAN

I'm gonna help by finding another way out.

ZACH

There is no other way out.

BRIAN

You're right, let's go back to negotiating with the monster. Hey, maniac! How about one more victim? Will that be

BRIAN (CONT'D)

enough for you?? Help me look, guys. There might be a vent or a crawlspace or--

(One pound on the door.)

BRIAN

What does that mean?

AMBER

I think I know. If we give you one more of us, you'll let the other two go?

(One pound on the door.)

ZACH

I guess he can be reasoned with.

BRIAN

... ... I bet you could outsmart him, Zach.

ZACH

Excuse me?

BRIAN

Here.

(HE grabs a fireplace poker.)

Take one of these with you and hold him off for a little bit. You're resourceful, you're fast.

ZACH

You think I should be the one who goes?

AMBER

Well ... we're in love.

ZACH

So what?

BRIAN

To choose one of us to be ... to be sent out to him, I
mean, you might well as choose both of us.

ZACH

Fine by me.

AMBER

What's the matter with you?

ZACH

I don't wanna be killed, Amber. That's my affliction.

BRIAN

You want us both dead?

ZACH

You're the ones who wanna go out and face a Zlatove
together. One or both, it doesn't matter to me.

BRIAN

I can't believe you would--

AMBER

What's a Zlatove?

ZACH

It's a, um ... it's a creature from another dimension. I don't
know if that's what that thing is, but it sure looks like one.
What? You've never heard of--?

AMBER

Of a Zlatove? No, nobody has but you. Are you responsible for
it being here?

ZACH

Just because a guy's read a few sci-fi books doesn't mean--

AMBER

Shut up. Brian, let's move that table.

BRIAN

What? No. We're not going out there.

AMBER

Of course we're not. We're throwing his ass out there.

ZACH

That's not a good idea.

BRIAN

What, are you best friends with it?

ZACH

I don't think that thing has any friends.

(A slam against the door.)

AMBER

Hey, Zlatove? Give us a minute. We're gonna toss Zach out, and then we're even. Move this on three. One, two--

ZACH

He doesn't know it was me who brought him here, otherwise he wouldn't have invited everybody from our house.
He probably just knows where the spell started.

BRIAN

You know how to do spells? What the fuck, man?

ZACH

He wants revenge on whoever disturbed him. If you push me
out there, with my dying breath I'll tell him I heard you both
saying the spell that brought him here.

AMBER

Well, we'll do the same to you then.

ZACH

I can tell him the specific words that I heard you say. Can you
do that?

(BRIAN grabs a fireplace poker.)

BRIAN

Maybe I just beat the shit out of you until you can't talk.

AMBER

Brian.

BRIAN

Throw your limp body out to him.

AMBER

Brian. He's not collecting the bodies. He wants revenge. He
wants to do it himself. Anything else would be useless.

(BRIAN tosses the fireplace poker in anger.)

ZACH

So which one of you is going?

AMBER

The minute we leave here, we're calling the cops on you.
Even before we call them on him.

BRIAN

Well, not "we."

AMBER

... ... I'm so sorry, Brian.

BRIAN

He should be apologizing, not you.

ZACH

I am sorry, if it makes any difference.

AMBER

It doesn't.

BRIAN

Whichever one of us survives, that one has to swear to fuck up his life forever.

AMBER

Deal.

(THEY embrace.)

ZACH

Leave him waiting too long, he might just take you both.

BRIAN

Shut up, asshole! I can't do this. I can't decide which--

AMBER

Let's let fate decide.

BRIAN

What do you mean?

AMBER

We go out together. Not to both be killed, but ... I don't know where he's standing. We walk out together, if he's on the left, he takes that person, if he's on the right, the

AMBER (CONT'D)

other. Whoever survives, fate decided it.

(BRIAN nods. THEY kiss, then break off.)

BRIAN

We're opening the door, dude. Get ready.

(THEY move the table, then open the door.
BRIAN exits but AMBER stays behind and
slams the door behind her. Pounding on
the door, then a scream, then silence.)

AMBER

(Under her breath)

I'm sorry, I'm sorry, I'm sorry.

ZACH

I think that was the smart move.

AMBER

I don't care what you think. His blood is on your hands, not
mine. ... ... Are you gonna go now?

ZACH

Ladies first.

AMBER

He said we'd be even, right?

ZACH

I mean, he banged on the door.

AMBER

But that was an agreement.

ZACH

Sure. But it occurs to me that something that could send us an intricate invitation to trap us could probably make an agreement out loud if he really meant it, right?

(One pound. Then more and more pounding. It keeps getting louder. End of play.)

THE GLORIOUS BLINDING LIGHT

adapted from the short story
"Three Body Problem"
by Charlie Franco

"The Glorious Blinding Light"
Cast of Characters

Kate
June's best friend, a woman in her 20s.

June
Kate's best friend, a woman in her 20s.

Zach
June and Kate's weed guy, indeterminate age.

Voice
A voice of authority from outside the cabin.

Place & Time

A vacation cabin, night.

Author's Notes

Please take any double ellipses (... ...) to mean a brief pause, not a hesitation in speech.

Overlaps are marked in Caryl Churchill's style of a slash (/) meaning the beginning of an overlap.

In the dark, a THUMP, then another THUMP, them a third THUMP, loud and heavy-sounding. Then the display lights of appliances appear on stage, along with the beeps and whirrs of them returning to life. Two figures are seen in silhouette on a couch, apart, breathing heavily.

KATE

June? I can't see anything.

JUNE

Power surge.

KATE

Is that all it was?

JUNE

It was part of it. Definitely not all of it.

KATE

It felt like more than that. ... ... I can't see any--

JUNE

There's a flashlight in the drawer.

KATE

What drawer?

JUNE

In the ... the thing. Next to you.

(JUNE reaches into the drawer of the nearby table. SHE gets out a flashlight and turns it on. KATE gets one too.)

KATE

You couldn't remember the word "table?"

      (SHE turns on her flashlight.)
      They're not very strong.

JUNE

The power's on. You can go flip the light switch.

KATE

So can you.

      (But THEY both don't move.)

KATE (CONT'D)

What happened?

JUNE

Something. I don't know.

KATE

Okay, but what do you think hap--?

JUNE

I think I was taken. It sounds stupid, but ... yeah. I think I was taken. Taken up.

KATE

... ... Me too.

JUNE

Or, I don't know, maybe we got dosed or something.

KATE

What, because I said I was too?

JUNE

No, it's ... we were just sitting here like this. The three of us had just smoked, and we were watching ... something when those lights filled the house.

KATE

I was in the kitchen.

JUNE

Those lights were so bright. Maybe they're testing some sort of weapon.

KATE

June, I was up getting us snacks. And you weren't sitting there either. You were on the other side of the couch. It wasn't a weapon they were-- I mean, who's they?

JUNE

You'd be surprised.

KATE

Enough of your conspiracy theory nonsense.

JUNE

Yeah, clearly this is a totally normal situation we're in and I'm overreacting.

KATE

We were taken up. Abducted. God, that word is so--

JUNE

What do you remember after the giant, bright light?

KATE

I remember the smell. It was sweet, like moss. But it made me wanna throw up.

JUNE

I don't remember any smell. Just the blinding light and then, and then I wasn't here anymore.

KATE

I remember something touching me. Something pushing into my stomach. Like a prodding. You?

JUNE
(Shaking her head)
I remember being covered in something wet, something thick and slimy. But I'm dry now. ... ... Were we dosed?

KATE

I didn't slip anything into your snacks. Jesus.

JUNE

Not you, Kate. Zach.

KATE

I don't think he'd do that. Where would he even get--?

JUNE

Well, I mean, he is a drug dealer. I don't ... Zach, where are you hiding? If you dosed us, so help me!

KATE

Just turn on the lights.

JUNE

You. If you're really not scared of--

KATE

I am scared. We weren't dosed. I think we were taken up. If you think we were, then what does it hurt to--?

(JUNE makes an annoyed sound and
hops up off the couch and turns
on the lights. We now see the body
of ZACH, on the floor, quite dead.
His shirt's pulled up, showing a
long clean incision on his stomach,
no stitches. KATE screams.)

JUNE

Stop. He's faking. You can get up now, you prick. We know
you laced those joints with ... something bad.

KATE

I think he's dead.

JUNE

He's not. Poke him. Like they poked you.

KATE

They prodded me.

JUNE

(Standing over ZACH)

I don't know the difference. Zach. Get up. Get up!!
(SHE pushes at his body with her
foot. SHE kicks him a little.)
Seriously, Zach, I know it's a fake. If that cut were real, it'd be
bleeding. ... ... Fine, I'll prove it.

(SHE puts her fingers on the
incision and her hand goes straight
in. SHE falls to her knees.)

KATE

Oh God, that is so gross!

117

JUNE

It's not. It's empty.

KATE

What do you mean?

JUNE

I mean, I should be feeling a stomach or something, right?

KATE

Intestines, I think. I was terrible at anatomy, though.

>(JUNE takes her hand out of ZACH.
>It's completely clean.)

JUNE

Well, I should have, you know, guts on my hand, right?

KATE

Check his pulse.

JUNE

He's empty, Kate.

KATE

I still think you should--

JUNE

Check it yourself, dude.

>(SHE gets up and moves away from ZACH,
>flexing her hand. KATE goes and checks
>ZACH's pulse. SHE shakes her head no.)

JUNE

Shocking.

KATE

I've never slept with a dead person before.

KATE (CONT'D)
(Off of JUNE's look)
I mean, nobody I've ever slept with has died.

JUNE
I just didn't know you'd slept with Zach.

KATE
Well, he's cute, and, um, funny, sweet. To be honest, I though we might have a future or ... probably for another time, huh? So who do we call?

JUNE
Um ... nobody?

KATE
We have to tell someone.

JUNE
Tell them what? Aliens killed our weed guy?? We don't even know what happened to us.

KATE
I think I was probed. But not, you know, the usual way. Just in my stomach.

JUNE
(Pointing to ZACH's stomach)
Do you have a ...?

KATE
Oh, God, I hadn't ...
(SHE pulls up her shirt a little
to check her stomach. Nothing.)
Well, that's something positive at least.

JUNE

My throat feels weird.

KATE

Like laryngitis or--

JUNE

I think they put something down it. I sorta remember that.

KATE

They didn't do that to me. Are you sure you were ... Do you think it was the same people?

JUNE

Do I think we got simultaneously abducted by different aliens? Chances seem low.

KATE

You don't have to be that--

JUNE

What are we going to do/ about Zach?

KATE

Stop interrupting me! You're always interrupting me!!

JUNE

... ... You through?
(Off KATE's nod)
What are we going to do about Zach?

KATE

We should get our stories straight.

JUNE

About getting abducted?

KATE

Yes. We choose one of our stories and, and, and both say that's what happened. Blinding light, prodded, probed, something in the stomach, then dropped back here. We found Zach and called the police immediately. ... ... What?

JUNE

We have to get rid of him.

KATE

No, we don't. Do you think they won't believe us?

JUNE

You don't believe me about my throat.

KATE

I mean, I feel like if someone put something in your throat, you wouldn't just think, you'd know.
(Off of JUNE's look)
We could call the paramedics and let them sort it out.

JUNE

Cool. Yeah, that's ... Why don't you do that. I'm gonna take off and let you handle it.

KATE

You can't go.

JUNE

Oh, I'm not going. Because I was never here. You're so gung-ho about telling someone, I'm not gonna stop you.

KATE

Look, I get that you're nervous, but ... but, I mean, how would we even get rid of him?

JUNE

There's a pond a quarter mile from here. We carry him--

KATE

For a quarter of a mile?

JUNE

Well, he's not that heavy anymore. We take him there, put some rocks inside of him, and then he's gone.

KATE

And if somebody asks about him?

JUNE

We tell the truth. He came here to my parents' cabin, sold us some weed, and then left. There's no lie there and ... I mean, honestly, who's gonna ask questions about Zach?
(KATE starts crying.)
What? Because you slept with him?

KATE

We might have had a future. But really I thought if I was ever part of a, a, an alien contact then it'd be lovely and wonderful and peaceful. Glorious wisdom from ancient civilizations across the galaxy. But what is this? We're hiding a body for some drunk and destructive jerks.

JUNE

You should look on the bright side.

KATE

What the hell is that?

JUNE

Humans may not be the worst things in the universe.

KATE

That's a bright side?? What if we're the best creatures around? What's the point of anything then?

JUNE

... ... Maybe they'll come back.

KATE

How are you this bad at cheering people up?

JUNE

Abductees, real credible alien abductees, it doesn't happen to them just once. They are chosen for a reason.

KATE

Again, this isn't doing me any good.

JUNE

The next time will be better. They chose us for a reason. They kept us alive, not Zach, for a reason. For all we know, they used Zach's organs to create a cure for everything that kills us.

KATE

They want to turn humans into immortals?

JUNE

They want to turn us into immortals. And then we can decide what to do with the rest of humanity.

KATE

I don't wanna be a guinea pig.

JUNE

Not true. You don't wanna be the guinea pig that gets the bad stuff and dies. Nobody does. But the guinea pig that gets the cure? You absolutely wanna be that guinea pig.

KATE

So ... so we should just wait for the blinding lights to come back?

JUNE

Absolutely. But in the meantime, we should get rid of Zach.

KATE

What does that have to do with this?

JUNE

Because if the Queen of the Universe comes over to your place, you don't leave the trash she dropped on the floor to shame her when she comes back. You throw it away.

KATE

... ... Zach wasn't trash. I might have loved him.

JUNE

You're right. He might be the gateway to immortality and we should honor him for that. But also, we really should toss his body in the lake.

> (KATE nods and THEY get on opposite
> sides of ZACH. THEY pick him up.)

KATE

Wow, he is light.

JUNE

Told ya.

> (Then a low hum of noise, which
> gets louder and higher.)

KATE

Is that ...? It is, isn't it??

> (White lights fill the room, blinding
> them, their faces filled with ecstasy.)

JUNE

Yes. The return of the glorious blinding light.

> (Then the white light is replaced with
> red and blue light. A voice on a PA
> is heard from outside.)

VOICE (OFF)

Is everything all right in there?

> (KATE and JUNE look at each other, confused.)

VOICE (OFF)

Your neighbors heard some screaming after the power surge, called the sheriff's office. We need to do a welfare check. Y'all okay in there?

> (KATE and JUNE look at ZACH. Then
> THEY look up. THEY wait. THEY
> hope. THEY pray. End of play.)

INHERITANCE

adapted from the short story
by Brandon Nolta

"Inheritance"
Cast of Characters

Bruegel

An elderly lawyer.

Hooded Figure

The Creature, the creation of Victor Frankenstein.

Place & Time

A pub in a village in Germany, night, three years after the death of Victor Frankenstein.

Author's Note

Please take any double ellipses (... ...) to mean a brief pause, not a hesitation in speech.

A tavern. BRUEGEL finishes his ale. HE reaches into his pocket and pulls out a few coins. HE looks around for the barmaid.

BRUEGEL

Greta? Greta??

(The sound of a door opening, then heavy footsteps. BRUEGEL looks down and reaches into his pocket for one more coin.)

I was wondering where you'd gotten to. I'd've sworn you were just--

(But HE stops when HE sees who is entering. A tall, large HOODED FIGURE. BRUEGEL stands up. Before HE can speak)

HOODED FIGURE

Do not cry out, Herr Bruegel. I mean you no harm, but I will cause it if needed. Do you understand?

BRUEGEL

(Quietly)

Yes.

(The HOODED FIGURE motions for BRUEGEL to sit, which HE does. The HOODED FIGURE takes off his hood. BRUEGEL shudders a bit when HE sees.)

HOODED FIGURE

I don't believe we've met before.

BRUEGEL

No.

HOODED FIGURE

But you know who I am?

BRUEGEL

Yes.

HOODED FIGURE

I've been told lawyers were chatty creatures, full of high sentence, but you're just saying "yes" and "no."

BRUEGEL

I'm worried for the barmaid.

HOODED FIGURE

She's fine. Passed out but fine. I've no quarrel with her, or with you, Herr Bruegel. I apologize for this unorthodox approach, but it's necessary. The ravages of my existence are obvious.

BRUEGEL

Perhaps you may have heard differently but I'm not a rich man. The little I have goes to--

HOODED FIGURE

I'm not here to rob you.

BRUEGEL

Then what do you want, Creature?

HOODED FIGURE

To hire you. Your reputation in matters of estate law and inheritance precedes you.

BRUEGEL
Tell me you haven't reproduced.

HOODED FIGURE
No, sir. Don't even know if I can. No, I wish to stake a claim to my father's estate.

>   (HE takes a pitcher and a tankard
>   and fills it up. HE holds up the
>   pitcher, offering)

Another?

>   (BRUEGEL is steaming mad. The HOODED
>   FIGURE shrugs and drinks his drink.)

BRUEGEL
That you would ask such a thing, especially from someone who knew Victor Frankenstein as well as I, beggars belief.

HOODED FIGURE
Why should I not claim his property?

BRUEGEL
For starters, you are not his child.

HOODED FIGURE
He has no children.

BRUEGEL
He has no family at all. Because of you.

HOODED FIGURE
Don't believe everything you read.

BRUEGEL
For you to feel you have a claim on anything is preposterous. Seeing you here makes me--

HOODED FIGURE

Should his property be covered in ivy and occupied by rats and rabbits because you find me distasteful? I am Victor's creation. A singular offspring, alive because of his will and engineering. Any natural born child would say the same, were he to exist. But only I remain. Am I correct?

BRUEGEL

You are not ... wholly incorrect.

HOODED FIGURE

So you'll take my case, as they say?

BRUEGEL

You don't need me, Creature.

HOODED FIGURE

I've studied much since my rebirth, but law has not been one of the subjects.

BRUEGEL

I'm saying, just take it.

HOODED FIGURE

Take it?

BRUEGEL

Take the house. Take what's inside. Nobody has set foot in there in three years. After the stories that have been passed around about you, people have given the house such a wide berth, it's like you've been in there the whole time.
Why not make their ghost stories real and just take up residence?

HOODED FIGURE

... ... No, that won't do.

BRUEGEL

Whyever not?

HOODED FIGURE

Ivy goes up fast when a torch is put to it. People might try to exorcise the ghost using earthly means.

BRUEGEL

Then sack the house. Take the--

HOODED FIGURE

I came to you for legal advice. Can I inherit my father's estate?

BRUEGEL

And if you can't, how will you pay me for my legal opinions?

> (The HOODED FIGURE puts one finger up.
> HE finishes his ale and exits. BRUEGEL
> looks at the door, considers it, and then
> pours himself another drink. HE's a bit
> intrigued. The HOODED FIGURE returns
> with an iron trunk. It looks heavy but
> the HOODED FIGURE carries it like it's
> filled with feathers. HE tosses it with
> a heavy thunk in front of BRUEGEL.
> BRUEGEL kneels down and opens it. The
> expression on his face shows that it
> is full of gold.)

HOODED FIGURE

I don't need his money. I need his library and his research. And a place where I will not be bothered to study them. His estate, my birthplace, would be a refuge.

BRUEGEL

How did you get all this?

HOODED FIGURE

All that matters is that it's here now. And that I can pay you handsomely for your work. You say you're not a rich man? How would you like to be?

(BRUEGEL shakes his head and laughs softly, surprising himself. HE is really considering this now.)

BRUEGEL

... ... What you ask is--

HOODED FIGURE

No, sir. What I demand.

BRUEGEL

It's not impossible. It would involve ...

(HE laughs a little more now.)

HOODED FIGURE

What amuses you so?

BRUEGEL

The irony. Or the echo. Or whatever a poet might call it.

HOODED FIGURE

There's little poetry in me. Tell me.

BRUEGEL

We would need to create a new person.

(A weight silence, then a hearty laugh from the HOODED FIGURE.)

HOODED FIGURE

You almost had me there.

BRUEGEL

I only mean it legally. We need to have an heir that the courts would recognize. Find a woman of low reputation, have her describe an encounter with Victor when he was a young man, produce a youth who could be the result of that encounter, and have him make a claim to the inheritance.

HOODED FIGURE

And would the magistrate believe this story?

BRUEGEL

I think he would be happy to grant the entire Frankenstein estate to anyone who wanted it, even if it were a whore's bastard. I don't believe anyone would protest.

HOODED FIGURE

You still have a keen legal mind, Herr Breugel. Age has not dulled you.

BRUEGEL

If only my body were as sharp an instrument. Ah well, nothing to be done about that. So there, Creature, for your impossible problem I have given you a possible solution.

HOODED FIGURE

You believe a pair could be found who would play along with this ruse?

BRUEGEL

Go to the darker corners of any village in these parts. I'm sure you can find two who will be willing for the right price.

HOODED FIGURE

I'm sure you can. People see my face before they see the coins I have to offer.

BRUEGEL

I've given you advice, but now you're asking me to commit crimes.

HOODED FIGURE

So then your fee goes up?

BRUEGEL

You've received my counsel. That's as far as I can go. I must be getting home.

HOODED FIGURE

Your wife is waiting for you?

BRUEGEL

She will be if I'm much longer.

HOODED FIGURE

Victor always remembered the pies she made. Thought they were better than his mother's, though he'd never tell her that.

BRUEGEL

Why did he tell you?

HOODED FIGURE

He didn't. It's ... are any of your children lawyers as well, Herr Bruegel?

BRUEGEL

My eldest.

HOODED FIGURE

Took to it naturally, I imagine. Passed on from father to son.
Did you know my father was experimenting with that too?

BRUEGEL

I took no interest in Victor's unholy science.

HOODED FIGURE

He saw how certain instincts were passed on through biological process from parent to child and expanded on those. If instincts, then why not also thoughts and memories? A sturdy hypodermic syringe, a detailed knowledge of the brain's peculiar geography, and--

BRUEGEL

So you've already been through his research then.

HOODED FIGURE

No. The days we sat in the cold, before he passed into delirium and death, he told me of this. Was even able to demonstrate it. He didn't tell me about your wife's cooking, he ... passed it down to me.

BRUEGEL

No good comes of this work.

HOODED FIGURE

Not yet. But were I to claim my inheritance ...

BRUEGEL
(Getting up)

I must go.

HOODED FIGURE

You should stay.

BRUEGEL

My legs aren't what they used to be, but I know this village better than you. I know dark corners you'd never find.

HOODED FIGURE

But I know where you live. Where your wife sleeps.

(BRUEGEL doesn't move, just slumps
a bit, giving up.)

HOODED FIGURE (CONT'D)

Good. Once you've found this pair, these new heirs, you would handle the papers, the court proceedings, all of it?

BRUEGEL

It's not a good idea.

HOODED FIGURE

It was your idea.

BRUEGEL

It was a passing fancy. And your peculiar presence makes it impossible.

HOODED FIGURE

Why?

BRUEGEL

You would what? Act as the tutor for this youth? People would talk and you would be found out. Or you'd hide in the shadows of the home? But then what would stop this already unscrupulous pair from demanding more money to keep from exposing you? Or selling the house and keeping the money for themselves?

HOODED FIGURE

I would stop them.

BRUEGEL

And if they call your bluff, then you ... do what you've always done, and you're left in the same predicament as you are now.

HOODED FIGURE

I think that--

BRUEGEL

Sack the library, collect what you need, and use your money to purchase a secluded estate for yourself. I can assist you with that.

HOODED FIGURE

Don't interrupt me again.

BRUEGEL

Why not? You are an interruption. To my evening, to the natural course of life.

HOODED FIGURE

I would not need long in that lab. My father's work was--

BRUEGEL

Please stop calling him that.

HOODED FIGURE

Was nearly complete. The process need not be for one snatch of memory. It could be a complete transference. From one living brain to a relatively fresh donor.

BRUEGEL

So our fictitious heir ...

HOODED FIGURE

Will quickly be legitimate. I can shed all this hodgepodge of flesh and become reborn. Again.

BRUEGEL

You're asking me to be complicit to fraud and murder.

HOODED FIGURE

But the rightful heir will be receiving the Frankenstein estate. You have found a loophole in order to administer justice.

BRUEGEL

I have no interest.

(HE walks to the door.)

My wife and I are old. If your threat is death, a slow death, even that will be brief. I will not help you, Creature.

HOODED FIGURE

My threat is to wait until my father's research is complete. And then kill you and use your fresh brain to transfer myself to your body. And then to give your wife a slow death at your own hands.

BRUEGEL

... ... You are an abomination.

HOODED FIGURE

I am my father's son. Will you help me?

BRUEGEL

Have I any other choice?

HOODED FIGURE

Do this well and I will have more to offer than money.

BRUEGEL

I don't want what you're selling, Creature.

HOODED FIGURE

Why let this keen legal mind rot in unsteady flesh? A bit more time researching and you'll be able to pass all you've acquired on to a new, sturdier form. I will help you manage your inheritance.

> (The HOODED FIGURE pours ale into his tankard then offers it to BRUEGEL, who nods. The HOODED FIGURE fills up his tankard as lights down.)

LOOP GIRL

adapted from the short story "Estate"
by David Mathew

"Loop Girl"
Cast of Characters

Doctor

A police doctor in his early 50s.

Cora (15)

A young teenage girl in a terrible situation.

Cora (22)

The same woman at 22 in the same terrible situation.

Ops

The voice of the Police Operations center.

Place & Time

The townhouse where Cora has been put, evening, the near future.

Author's Notes

The Coras can be played by the same actor, with a bit of quick makeup and styling, or different actors who look alike.

Please take any double ellipses (... ...) to mean a brief pause, not a hesitation in speech.

Lights up on the stoop, front door and front room of a townhouse in profile. The DOCTOR, in police uniform, enters on the stoop side, holding a communicator of sorts. Not a walkie-talkie; we're a bit past that, time-wise.

DOCTOR

Ops, I'm at the Lancot Street address.

OPS (ON COMMUNICATOR)

Back-up is on the way, Doc. Three minutes out.

DOCTOR

Going to assess before he gets here.

OPS (ON COMMUNICATOR)

If parents are present, do not engage.

DOCTOR

Roger that. Over.

(HE goes to the door and knocks.
CORA, maybe fifteen, enters on
the front room side. SHE looks concerned.)

CORA (15)

Password?

DOCTOR

What?

(SHE's unsure. SHE puts on the
chain and opens the door.)

CORA (15)

Can I help you?

>(The DOCTOR holds up his badge.
HE looks into the house.)

DOCTOR

Are your parents home?

CORA (15)

Why?

DOCTOR

We had a call about a baby screaming last night.

CORA (15)

Did you get lost?

DOCTOR

Excuse me?

CORA (15)

A baby screaming last night? It's nearly dinner time.

DOCTOR

We got a call today about it. I got here when I could.

CORA (15)

Well, listen ...

>(But SHE stops and just stares
at him. HE's a little unnerved
by the pause.)

DOCTOR

Are you all right?

CORA (15)

You hear that? No baby screaming. Are we good?

DOCTOR

I think I asked if your parents are home.

CORA (15)

No, they're not.

DOCTOR

When will they be here? I'd like a word.

CORA (15)

They don't live here.

DOCTOR

You live alone?

(HE tries to look in again.)

DOCTOR (CONT'D)

How old are you?

CORA (15)

Is it a crime to live alone?

DOCTOR

Depends on how old you are.

CORA (15)

How old do I need to be to make it legal?

DOCTOR

Hey, kid, I've been on shift for about eleven hours straight, so maybe you do me a favor and lose the attitude.

CORA (15)

I'm eighteen.

DOCTOR

You don't look eighteen.

> CORA (15)
> (Under her breath)

Just wait.

> DOCTOR

What was that?

> CORA (15)

I'm underweight. Been on a diet for a modeling job, if you must know. Some people like that adolescent look. Is that against the law?

> DOCTOR

I'm not the law.

> CORA (15)

Your badge says police.

> (HE holds it up again, underlining
> it with his finger.)

> DOCTOR

Police doctor.

> CORA (15)

You sure didn't make that clear when you flashed it.

> DOCTOR

Tell me what's wrong with your baby.

> (CORA (15) slams the door on him. SHE
> exits to the rest of the house.
> HE takes a step back from the door
> and sits on the stoop. HE presses on
> his communicator.)

DOCTOR (CONT'D)

Lancot looks like a false alarm. What's the name and address on the call, so I can follow up?

OPS (ON COMMUNICATOR)

Anonymous call. Young girl, by the sound of it. Did you get a look at the baby?

DOCTOR

No.

OPS (ON COMMUNICATOR)

Signs of neglect? Soiled diapers, dirty dishes?

DOCTOR

No, it looked pretty clean in there. What happened to the backup?

OPS (ON COMMUNICATOR)

Got called in on a hostage situation. Some joker took some PCP and freaked out when his Loop Girl started changing.

DOCTOR

Tell him to just wait.

(Something has struck him, but HE
can't quite get it. OPS laughs.)

OPS (ON COMMUNICATOR)

Exactly. You're good for tonight, Doc. Head home. Over.

(HE gets up from the step and goes.
Lighting change. It's later, darker, the sun is
down. The DOCTOR enters, goes to the door,
and knocks. A WOMAN enters from the house.
SHE looks like CORA will at age 22, but she's
wearing the same clothes as CORA.)

149

> CORA (22)

Password?

> DOCTOR

I won't ask to talk to your parents. They don't live here.

> CORA (22)

As I said before.

> DOCTOR

Nor does a baby.

> CORA (22)

As I said before.

> DOCTOR

You didn't actually. Just slammed the door in my face. Wanna know how I know you don't have a baby?

(SHE opens the door, chain on.)

> CORA (22)

Oh, I'll sob if you don't tell me.

> DOCTOR

No toys, no crib, no stroller. I mean, you could have them in the back, but that stuff spreads out. This place is pristine. ... ... You look different.

> CORA (22)

Changed my hair.

> DOCTOR

Sure. That's what it is. You called it in, right?

> CORA (22)

Called what in?

DOCTOR

Child at risk. Why I'm here. You called it in. So can you let me in now?

CORA (22)

You're a doctor. I'm not sick.

DOCTOR

You will be in about five, six hours, I bet. You're getting older by the minute.

CORA (22)

So are you.

DOCTOR

Not the way you are. I'm not a Loop Girl, am I?

CORA (22)
(A frown, then)
I don't know what you're talking about. You should go.

DOCTOR

Before the change goes to more than your hair? My guess is you'll be older than me in a few hours. I know it speeds up as you get older. An old lady by midnight, and then a baby again. On a loop.

(SHE exhales takes off the chain, opens the door, and walks away. The DOCTOR enters, closing the door behind him.)

CORA (22)

How do you know about all this?

DOCTOR

There are things flatfoots in uniform can't understand these days. Higher-ups don't want them screwing up and busting your guys, so they've asked some of us discrete medical professionals to help with any problems.

CORA (22)

So they knew I was--?

DOCTOR

No, we get called for regular old neglected babies too. That's what the police think this is. I can help you with whoever you're running from.

CORA (22)

What makes you think I'm running?

DOCTOR

Some guys who are with Loop Girls sell them by the hour to other men. The sort of men who'd like an eighty year-old. The sort of men who'd like an eight year-old too.

CORA (22)

No, you've got that all wrong. My man and I, it's just us.

DOCTOR

Yeah, then why do you ask for a password? How many guys come over?

CORA (22)

You don't understand.

DOCTOR

Maybe you don't now. But when you made the call--

CORA (22)

I don't remember making any call.

DOCTOR

My guess? Cry for help. When you were a kid this afternoon you pretended to be your neighbor, called in about a baby screaming so that it'd bring the cops.

CORA (22)

Why on Earth would I do that?

DOCTOR

Maybe you'd just been with a guy who thinks an eight year-old is too old. Didn't wanna face the darkness again.

CORA (22)

What'll you do?

DOCTOR

Wait until your man comes back here and take him in. Being a pimp's still illegal.

CORA (22)

I was made for him.

DOCTOR

I'm aware.

CORA (22)

Isn't that slavery?

DOCTOR

You can't ... it doesn't work that way.

CORA (22)

So I'm a person for one law but I'm not for another.

DOCTOR

We're still working out all the kinks.

CORA (22)

What are *your* kinks? Eight or eighty?

DOCTOR

About *forty*-eight, I'd say.

CORA (22)

So you wanna hang out and wait a couple of hours?

DOCTOR

I can help you.

CORA (22)

I don't need help.

DOCTOR

The you of this afternoon thinks differently.

CORA (22)

What do kids know?
                    (SHE takes him in.)
Forty-eight? You like older women?

DOCTOR

I'm fifty-one.

CORA (22)

You don't look it. You really could come back in a few hours.
I'll give you the password and everything.

DOCTOR

Why are you acting this way?
                    (Looking around)
Does he have cameras set up?

CORA (22)

This is just the part of the day where I start to accept my fate. Try to make the best of it.

DOCTOR

It doesn't have to be that way. He's breaking the law. I can call in for--

CORA (22)

Why do we exist? Girls like me?

DOCTOR

That answer's a little above my pay grade.

CORA (22)

I'm not asking for philosophy. Just pure commerce. What were we created to do? It's not like I was told.

DOCTOR

Oh. Provide companionship for those who, um ... might cause trouble for, uh, re--human women.

CORA (22)

You were gonna say real women, right?
(Off his shrug)
Who cares if they're selling us to each other?

DOCTOR

The hope is that looping means you can gradually transition them to a more appropriate age. As they see you change, the desire ... moves.

CORA (22)

That was the plan? Turn creeps and pedophiles into upstanding citizens? You created a harem of us and expected them to stay monogamous?

DOCTOR

I'm not ... I didn't invent you. I'm just here to help.

CORA (22)
(Bursting into tears)

Take me from him then, Doctor.

> (SHE goes and embraces him.
> HE puts his arms around her.)

DOCTOR

Good. Yes. I can do that. I can protect you and--

CORA (22)
(Her face close to his)

And then set me free? So I never have to do this again. Can you do that?

DOCTOR

... ... Well, I can, I can talk to somebody about, uh ...

> (SHE steps away from him, all the
> "hysterics" gone.)

CORA

That's what I thought.

DOCTOR

Like I said, I'm not the law.

CORA

Just a person. A real person. Aren't you special?

> (SHE goes to the door and holds it
> open for him. HE leaves the house
> but turns back to her on the stoop.)

CORA (CONT'D)

Dolly. When you come back, and I bet you will, the password's
Dolly.

> (SHE closes the door on him. HE
> wants to say something, but goes,
> head heavy. Lights down. End of play.)

THIS IS GOING
TO KEEP HAPPENING, ISN'T IT?

<u>This Is Going To Keep Happening, Isn't It</u>
Cast of Characters

Freddy

Twenties, kind of shy and dumpy, in love with Maxine.

Maxine

Twenties, future med student, strong but sometimes doubting herself.

Tim

Twenties, Maxine's boyfriend, a little snarky.

Fred

Freddy twenty-five years later, very handsome and confident.

Timothy

A man in his seventies (is he Tim fifty years later?), played by the actor playing Tim.

Place & Time

One night, inside and outside Freddy's apartment.

Author's Note

Please take any double ellipses (... ...) to mean a brief pause, not a hesitation in speech.

Lights up on one half a split stage, the sidewalk outside Freddy's apartment, right near a bus stop. FREDDY is with MAXINE.

FREDDY

So ... yeah, I mean, that's it. I knew I had to tell you how I feel or ... or this is going to keep happening, isn't it? I couldn't just keep it, um, you know, bottled up.

MAXINE

... Why the hell not, Freddy?

FREDDY

Well, I've been feeling this way for a while and--

MAXINE

So all the time we've done stuff as friends, when you've given me advice about me and Tim, whether we should break up, it's all because you've been secretly in love with me?

FREDDY

Not just that, and I didn't know how I felt until I--

MAXINE

And to do this on a night when we're going out for drinks to celebrate ... did you expect me to get drunk and then fall into your arms after this declaration?

FREDDY

No, Maxine, I wasn't trying to-- I just felt the need to--

MAXINE

You should have kept that need to yourself. 'night.

(SHE exits.)

FREDDY

Shit. Shit, shit, shit. Why'd you think she'd actually be interested in you, you ...

(HE exits. A giant WHOOSH like a jet plane.)

FREDDY (OFF)

What the hell?

(Lights down on the street and up on
the other side of the stage, the apartment.
FREDDY enters. FRED is there waiting.)

FREDDY

Dude, did you just hear that weird jet sound?

FRED

Good, you're home.

FREDDY

Oh, sorry. I thought you were my roommate, I didn't know he had a ... is there a problem with him?

FRED

He's gone for the weekend, isn't he? I'm here to see you.

FREDDY

How did you even get in here?

FRED

I had the key. Still. Because I'm you, Freddy.

FREDDY

... ... Okay. Sure.

(FREDDY goes to the door to leave.)

FRED

No, don't go. I, God, right: El Paso, Texas.

FREDDY
(Stopping)
What the hell is this?

FRED
It's ridiculous, because I couldn't remember if we changed the code words after what happened earlier tonight, or if we just said, fuck it, use it for inspiration.

FREDDY
Why did you say that city to me?

FRED
Because it's the phrase I promised I'd use if I ever met myself traveling through time, to know it was me.

FREDDY
No, no, no, no, no.

FRED
Do you think other people think like we do, have a code word like that? I mean, they'll have to, going forward, but right now we're pretty alone in this.

FREDDY
You don't look anything like me.

FRED
I look better than you, you mean.

FREDDY
That's not what I was--

FRED
Well, you get older, you get very, very rich, you get a trainer, you get plastic surgery, and now this handsome face I'm wearing is the one you present to the world.

FREDDY

Very, very rich?

FRED

Inventing time travel is fairly lucrative. And it's not even the thing that's made you the most money.

FREDDY

... I'm just supposed to take you at your word that you're me from the future?

FRED

You're supposed to take me at your words. El Paso, Texas. Ever tell anybody about that? No, we haven't.

FREDDY

Assuming I believe you, then--

FRED

No assumptions needed.

       (Presenting a piece of paper to him)

I have proof.

       (Lights down on the apartment and up
       on the street. MAXINE has returned
       and SHE's on her phone. We see TIM
       in a special, on his phone.)

TIM

Hey, Max, still celebrating?

MAXINE

Not, um, not really. I'm gonna come over if that's cool

TIM

Oh, okay. Sure. You gotta take the bus, though, 'cause the trains aren't running. ... ... If you don't mind, is everything all right?

MAXINE

Yeah, Tim, not really. Freddy used the night of my celebration of getting into med school to barf out all his feelings on my shoes and tell me he loves me.

TIM

Which you already knew because I told you.

MAXINE

Which I already knew because I'm smart enough to get into med school.

TIM

Not without Freddy's help.

MAXINE

Dick. Correct, but still a dick.

TIM

If you don't mind, what did you do?

MAXINE

I unloaded on him. Why couldn't he just get over me alone? I made him feel shitty and now I'm gonna apologize.

TIM

Why?

MAXINE

Because I feel shitty.

TIM

You don't have to do this. He hijacked your night.

MAXINE

I'll do it from the intercom. He probably won't even let me up. Then I'll jump on the crosstown bus and hang out right after. Love you, Timmy.

TIM

Love you too, Max.

(SHE hangs up and presses the intercom.)

FREDDY (ON INTERCOM)

Hey, Maxine. Come on up.

MAXINE

How'd you know it was ... Freddy, I just wanted to say that you didn't deserve for me to treat you--

FREDDY (ON INTERCOM)

Seriously, come up. There's someone you gotta meet.

(Lights down on the street then up
on the apartment. It's later. All
THREE are smiling and drinking.)

FRED

No, no, no, you can't ask me that.

MAXINE

Look, if I knew when the Steelers were gonna win and when they were gonna lose, it would take a lot of anxiety out of watching the games.

FREDDY

It would take the excitement out too, right?

MAXINE

Excitement's overrated. Reducing anxiety is where it's at.
(Sound of a text. SHE checks.)
Ignoring you, Tim, sorry. This is a little bit more important.
So, um ... why are you here, future Freddy?

FRED

Just Fred is fine.

MAXINE

Here to warn us that in the future our kids are assholes?

FRED

Kids? You two don't have kids.

FREDDY

She's referencing "Back to the--

FRED

If you had kids, I wouldn't be able to do this. Excuse me.
Don't worry, I know where the bathroom is.

(HE exits. A pause, then)

MAXINE

Hey, Freddy, if this is all like a big joke for my amusement,
I mean, I'm impressed, but you got me. You can call it off
whenever you want.

FREDDY

If it's a joke, it's a joke on me too. Look at this.
(Showing her the paper)
He brought with him a list of every email I'm going to get
today. Sender, subject line, time stamp. Even the spam ones.
In fact, there should be one from Verizon coming ...
(Ding of an email.)
Look at my laptop, Maxine. It's crazy but it's real.

(FRED returns.)

MAXINE

I can't believe you didn't call the police on him.

FRED

I told him the magic words: El Paso, Texas.

MAXINE

Where my grandparents lived?

FREDDY

It's something I kept in my head as a kind of password. The way you talked about it, the mountains slowly appearing in the west, it just felt like a safe place to be. He told me you were coming too. I can't see the front of the building from here, but–

MAXINE

What happened last time? The first time?

FRED

Oh, well, you apologized, I muttered, "Okay, fine, thanks," and then got drunk alone and binge watched a terrible sit-com called "Substitute Bailiff." But that weekend, this week-end, I started to get some ideas which, brick by brick, would lead me to this process.

MAXINE

So our awkward evening means you get to visit dinosaur times and Gatsby-type flapper parties? Not a bad trade.

FRED

No. No, this, tonight, is as far back as I can go.

FREDDY

So I invented shitty time travel?

FRED

You figured out the inherent problem, kid. If you traveled back too far, you say the wrong word to somebody, suddenly your parents don't meet and time travel doesn't get invented.

FRED (CONT'D)

Tonight's the night Freddy stops obsessing over Maxine and focuses on other things. Because you two won't be together, time travel is inevitable from now on.

FREDDY

Wow.

FRED

Don't mean for it to sound so portentous, but that's the way it goes in all things space and time.

FREDDY

I mean who can say what kind of relationships any of us--?

FRED

I'm from the future, so I can say. It can't happen between you two. The end.

MAXINE

This is ... wow, is right. Excuse me.
(SHE starts to exit.)
You really look like this in the future?

FRED

It's amazing what money can do, isn't it?

(SHE exits.)

FREDDY

That is a ... that is an amazing story.

FRED

Yeah, it is. You think she's buying it?

FREDDY

Excuse me?

FRED

Do you think it's working? The whole "this can never be because it will destroy the path of progress" angle? There's nothing more enticing than forbidden fruit.

FREDDY

Wait, is that not true?

FRED

Parts are true. You did invent time travel after all.

FREDDY

Yeah, but about the limits on it. Are they--?

FRED

Maybe it's better that you don't know. Just let her fall for me as what could be.

FREDDY

Did you plan this all to make her interested in me? Are you even really what I look like in the future?

FRED

If I tell you, will you blurt it out, or "can you keep it, um, you know, bottled up?" Let me handle this, kid.

> (Lights down on the apartment and up on the street, later. TIMOTHY, an older man is at the bus stop. MAXINE enters and stands waiting for the bus, a smile on her face.)

TIMOTHY

I'm sure it'll be here any minute.
(Off of her nod.)
If you don't mind, the smile on your face tells me you had a really fun night. Out celebrating?

MAXINE

Yeah. And it was a night that would make your head spin.

TIMOTHY

Those are good to have. At my age I look back on those nights as these little wonderful anomalies.

MAXINE

Yeah, well ... honestly, it might be more than that. It might be a life-changing night.

TIMOTHY

Were you proposed to? Is there a ring you're hiding?

MAXINE

No, it's ... a path I never considered may be, uh ... it may be the perfect path for me.

TIMOTHY

All laid out for you with a treasure chest at the end?

MAXINE

I mean, you're not totally wrong.

TIMOTHY

Again, if you don't mind a little advice: any path like that is a lie.

MAXINE

This is a little more than "all that glitters isn't gold."

TIMOTHY

The point of life is uncertainty. It's how you deal with what comes across your path that tells you who you are.

MAXINE

Excitement's overrated. Reducing anxiety is where it's at.

TIMOTHY

What were you celebrating? That was excitement, wasn't it?

MAXINE

I got into med school. I'm gonna be a doctor.

TIMOTHY

What's the path then? A residency and a job all lined up?

MAXINE

No. More of a relationship thing. Maybe I need a change.

TIMOTHY

From what I hear, new doctors have no time for anything but their work. If you don't mind my--

MAXINE

Maybe I do mind. Maybe you should mind your own business.

TIMOTHY

If somebody shows you no concern, hijacks your night and barfs their feelings all over your shoes, time won't change them.

MAXINE

He didn't really-- How did you know that?
          (The sound of the bus arriving.)
Tim? Tim, is that you?

TIMOTHY

Whatever you're thinking about doing, give it a night to think it over.

MAXINE

I can't believe this. You traveled back in time to win me back? I ... Oh God. This is going to keep happening, isn't it?

TIMOTHY

Please don't leave me again, Max.

> (SHE runs away.)

Please!

> (Lights down. End of play.)

ZEE

adapted from the short story "Zee"
by Leea Glasheen

"Zee"
Cast of Characters

She
A woman in her mid twenties, Guy's roommate.

Zee
A glorious cosmic being of no apparent gender or origin.

Guy
A man in his late twenties, She's roommate

Place & Time

The apartment where Guy and She live, Saturday morning, and a corner of space removed from time.

Author's Notes

Please take any double ellipses (... ...) to mean a brief pause, not a hesitation in speech.

> Lights up on SHE in her living room.
> SHE's putting down a basket of laundry to fold. SHE folds one t-shirt and then notices a bowl of strange candy on the coffee table. SHE calls to her roommate.

SHE

Hey, Guy? This candy yours?
> (No answer)
Mind if I have some?

> (No answer. SHE shrugs and picks up one
> and tosses it in the air, trying to catch
> it in her mouth. SHE fails. SHE tries
> again. Fails. SHE shrugs and grabs a
> handful and puts them in her mouth. SHE
> takes two bites and then chokes. SHE
> passes out on the floor. Quick light
> change. Single special on SHE. SHE sits
> up and spits the candy out into her hand.
> In darkness, the voice of ZEE.)

ZEE

Feel better?

SHE

Yeah, I ... what's happening?

> (In another area, ZEE appears. ZEE is
> a glorious cosmic being of no apparent
> gender or origin.)

ZEE

That candy was a gift to bring you here. Welcome! Time for us to have a talk.

SHE

Who are you? What is--

ZEE

We are everything good.

SHE

We: you and me? Or is this a royal "we"?

ZEE

We are only speaking of ourselves.

SHE

That ... doesn't really help.

ZEE

(Gesturing only to ZEE)

We are everything good.

SHE

You're God?

ZEE

If you like. You may refer to us as Zee, if you feel you need to put a name on us, which you most certainly do not and should not, but you may choose what you like. We are all about choice, you see. Democracy not autocracy.

SHE

Okay. Am I dead, Zee?

ZEE

Even after all that you still call me ...? Ah, well. Dead? No. Not
yet. In-between right now. Everyone has this moment, this
crossroads, and this is yours.

SHE

Everyone has a moment?

ZEE

We have said it and therefore it is truth. We know all and see
all.

SHE

Every single person? Five billion people and each one has--

ZEE

We do not live in time and space as you do. We are giving this
moment to thousands of people as we speak.

SHE

That wasn't my point. I feel like this'd mean that everybody
has near death experiences where they meet God.
That seems bananas. People would talk about that.

ZEE

We do not allow them to remember. Were there proof of us,
choice would go away. One does not choose to believe in grav-
ity, it just is. We must preserve choice.

SHE

So I can choose to remember this when it's over?

ZEE

... ... This is your crossroads. Your life stretches out before you
with but two choices, our way or the way of the Deceiver.

                         SHE

Meaning, like, the devil? That's really for real?

                         ZEE

Satan, yes, the Deceiver. We call him that because with all the
beauty in the world that we've created, following him would
be giving in to deception. You understand, don't you, my
child?

                         SHE

I'm not a child.

                         ZEE

We are aware. It is a term of endearment.

                         SHE

Calling someone "childish" isn't endearing.

                         ZEE

We were not--
              (Stopping themself and refocusing)
Tell us what you love about our world. The adorable animals,
the verdant pastures, the--

                         SHE

Are you open to questions, or is it just "me or the other guy?"

                         ZEE

This is happening.
              (Off her reaction)
You seem to not be taking this seriously. This is not a halluci-
nation caused by a brain starved of oxygen. We are happy to
answer questions, but the choice is all.

                         SHE

Okay. ... ... Why do smart animals taste delicious?

ZEE

What?

SHE

It feels like, morally speaking, that there shouldn't be any incentive to kill and eat something that's been given intelligence. If pigs and octopuses tasted terrible, nobody would eat them. Feels like that's something you could choose.

ZEE

All things are part of our plan.

SHE

But is it a good plan?

ZEE

It is our plan, so by definition it is good. We know all and see all. But we will take down your remarks.
(ZEE produces a quill and scroll.
ZEE scribbles down a few words.)
Any other complaints?

SHE

I don't think that's a complaint. Just a question.

ZEE

You take issue with our plan?

SHE

I have some concerns.

ZEE
(Dispensing with the scroll)
Then we would call that a complaint. Do you have any more or are you ready to make your choice?

SHE

What happens if I don't go with you, Zee?

ZEE

Still with the ... then you live as a servant of the Deceiver and wait to see what happens once life leaves you.

SHE

So hell? You're threatening me with hell?

ZEE

We make no threats. We provide a choice. So what will you choose?

SHE

You're kinda obsessed with this, huh? I don't know if we're so free if it all comes down to one choice made one time, no takebacks. It all seems like a way to break me or make me your enemy.

ZEE
(Shrugging their shoulders)
You speak as if we enjoy this. We do it all for you. To teach you.

SHE

Some sort of additional tutorial might be helpful. Bare mins: a webinar or an FAQ.

(ZEE pops a truffle in their mouth.)

ZEE
(Speaking while chewing)
Serve us or serve that guy. Your choice.

SHE

Either way you win. More followers or more enemies to be better than.

ZEE

What about lilacs? What about stormy skies outside when
you're snuggled up cozily in a warm blanket? What about the
Alps? Have you seen the Alps?

SHE

What are you talking about?

ZEE

They're a mountain range in Europe, primarily--

SHE

I know about the Alps. Why are you bringing them up?

ZEE

Most people feel better when they count their blessings.

SHE

Is this a joke to you?

ZEE

We're trying to make you happy. We see you're not impressed.
We see that you might just be the biggest ingrate of all time.
Lilacs alone are a wonder to--

SHE

Lilacs are great, but how about some consistent peace and
joy? Is that too much to ask?

ZEE

We'll take that under advisement.

SHE

Yeah, I can see how seriously you're taking it.

ZEE

So you'll be following the Deceiver then?

SHE

Once I make a choice you send me back? Is that it?

ZEE

You are back, my silly, stupid child. Just open your eyes after you tell me which side you choose.

SHE

... ... Neither.

> (SHE shuts her eyes for a few seconds,
> then disappears from the spotlight.
> The lights change back to as they were
> at the start. SHE is on the floor,
> her eyes now open. SHE gets up and
> sees that ZEE is there watching.)

ZEE

What are you going to do? We're waiting.
> (SHE starts folding laundry.)
What are you going to do after the laundry is folded?

SHE

I'm ... I am going to be kind to the limit of my capacity, and when I find I'm being a selfish pig's ass, I'm going to try again.

ZEE

So you are going to do my work.

SHE

Nope. I'm doing my work.
> (Calling)
Guy? You around?

> (GUY, SHE's roommate, shambles in. HE
> is shaggy around the edges, but a decent
> fellow. HE's in a t-shirt and shorts.)

GUY

I heard something fall a few seconds ago. You okay?

SHE

(Handing him a shirt)

No worse for wear. I got one of your shirts by mistake.

GUY

Sweet, thanks. Who's that?

SHE

That's Zee. They're just visiting.

GUY

'sup Zee?

ZEE

Hello, my child. You'll remember none of this.

(GUY starts changing out of his old
shirt and into the clean one.)

GUY

That checks out.

SHE

Zee's just about to leave.

ZEE

We most certainly are not. Not until a choice has been made.

SHE

Well, I got shit to do, Zee, so it might be a while.

ZEE

Stop ignoring us!

SHE

I'm not ignoring you. I'm just not taking you into consideration. I'm not playing your game.

ZEE

You must choose.

SHE

I did. Just going to be compassionate because I decide to be.

ZEE

Everything you choose is because we lead you to choose it.

GUY

That doesn't sound like any choice at all then.
                    (Noticing the candy)
These yours? Can I have some?

SHE

Zee brought them. I'm sure they wouldn't mind sharing.

GUY

Cool.

            (GUY takes a handful of candy and pops
            it in his mouth.)

ZEE

If you do not choose, our wrath will hail down upon you.

SHE

Will you kill me?

ZEE

Our wrath is all powerful.

SHE

And then I'll get to choose heaven or hell?

ZEE

That's ... no, that's a choice you must make in life. It's meaningless if you do it at the end. Who wouldn't choose heaven then?

SHE

So you won't kill me.

GUY

You two want me to give you some privacy?

ZEE

Our wrath can be ... reined in a bit. So that you will not perish but suffer. What then?

SHE

I guess I'll suffer. Then I'll go back to what I'm doing.

ZEE

But in your heart you'll curse us. "What kind of a being would do this to me?" you'll say.

SHE

What I hear, it's part of a good plan. If I don't know what good and bad are anymore, how the hell could I choose?

ZEE

Yes, but what about me, er, us? What about us?

SHE

You do your thing, and I'll do mine.

ZEE
(A petulant child)
That's not-- You can't-- No! Noooo! Choose. CHOOSE!

GUY

(Taking another handful of candy)

These are really good? Are they British?

(SHE continues folding, and GUY
continues chewing. ZEE, furious,
tries to take the high road.)

ZEE

We are not pleased with you at all.

GUY

... Her or me?

ZEE

We will punish you until you beg to choose. And then we will
deny you your choice.

GUY

It's not worth it. When she makes up her mind, she's real
stubborn. You don't even know.

ZEE

We know all and see all.

SHE

Then how come you didn't know I wouldn't choose?

(ZEE breathes through their nose,
heavily, a few times, summoning
up all the rage in the universe,
then tamping it down again.)

ZEE

We will make you forget and we will return.

(All of the light in the world
fills up the stage, then darkness,
then back to normal with ZEE gone.)

SHE

That's amazing ... I didn't lose one sock. I'm on a great laundry streak. Want me to do yours?

GUY

Seriously? Cool. Thanks.

(Lights down. End of play.)

DAVID L. WILLIAMS is a graduate of the theatre department of Cornell University, where he was a four-time award winner in the Heerman's-McCalmon Playwriting contest, and received his MFA in playwriting from the University of Nebraska. He has written more than thirty plays and musicals, and his work has been produced across the United States and internationally in Australia, Italy, Canada, Denmark, Norway, and Lithuania. His most recent productions include the world premiere of his full-length play *The Starving* at Barter Theatre (Abingdon, VA) and the ATHE Award of Excellence in Playwriting winner *The Censor* at Throughline Theatre (Pittsburgh, PA). He lives in Bellefonte, Pennsylvania with his wonderful wife Kathleen and his amazing son Samuel. www.playwrightdavid.com